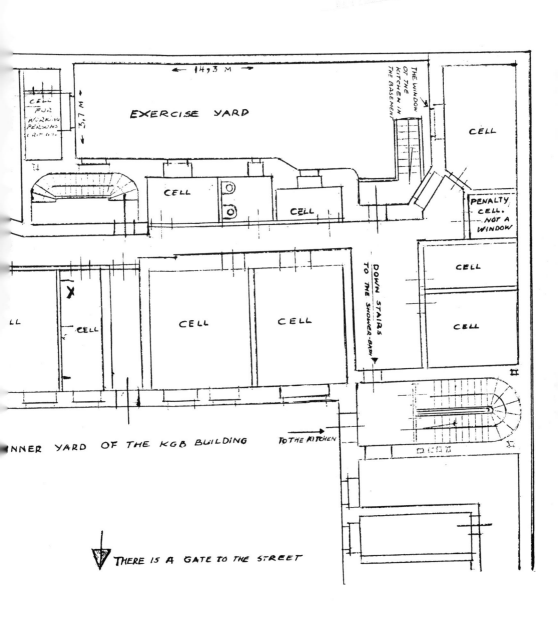

CELL FOR WORKING PERSONS [PRISONERS]

EXERCISE YARD

← 14,3 M →

3,7 M

THE WINDOW OF THE KITCHEN IN THE BASEMENT

CELL

CELL

CELL

PENALTY CELL. NOT A WINDOW

CELL

LL

CELL

CELL

CELL

DOWN STAIRS TO THE SHOWER-BATH

CELL

CELL

INNER YARD OF THE KGB BUILDING

TO THE KITCHEN

THERE IS A GATE TO THE STREET

WOMEN
IN
SOVIET
PRISONS

WOMEN IN SOVIET PRISONS

Helene Celmina

Illustrated by the author

Paragon House Publishers
New York

Published in the United States by
Paragon House Publishers
2 Hammarskjold Plaza
New York, New York 10017

Library of Congress Cataloging-in-Publication Data

Celmina, Helena.
  Women in Soviet Prisons.

  Translation of: Sievetes PSRS cietumos.
  1. Women prisoners—Soviet Union. 2. Prisons—Soviet
Union. 3. Political persecution—Latvia. I. Title.
HV9713.C4513   1985   365′.43′0947   85-21458
ISBN 0-913729-04-3

CONTENTS

FOREWORD

In 1977 during a private conversation, KGB Lieutenant-Colonel Kondratovs asked a Latvian émigré why she was so unhappy with the Soviet system. After all, she had a good job, a large income, an apartment, and even an automobile; everything a person could want. The woman never bothered to answer.

Helene Celmina, who survived four long years in the Soviet Gulag for the "crime" of reading foreign magazines, knew any answer would be superfluous. Because Kondratovs had to ask in the first place, he would never understand.

Instead, she took her experience to the West, to a world that not only understood, but highly valued personal freedom, legal justice, and human dignity. Other, more famous survivors of the Gulag have, of course, preceded her and have begun to unravel the curtain of secrecy shrouding the massive Soviet penal system. More will surely follow. What makes Helene Celmina's story so special however, is that it is a deeply personal one, focusing on the lives, experiences, and relationships of the women—mothers, wives, and daughters; murderesses, criminals, and thieves—she met, lived with, and worked with during her four years of imprisonment.

Although *Women in Soviet Prisons* is primarily about people, it can only be understood within its political context. To understand how a bright, young Latvian girl with a knack for languages and an insatiable desire to read, becomes, almost overnight, an "especially dangerous criminal to the state," one must understand what it means to be a Balt growing up in the Soviet Union.

Helene Celmina was born in 1929 in Latvia, a Baltic nation which gained its independence from tsarist Russia in 1918. Along with the neighboring countries of Lithuania and Estonia, Latvia struggled for centuries to free itself from the Russian empire and embraced its new sovereignty with enthusiasm. As a small but ancient culture whose Indo-European language was neither Slavic nor Teutonic, the Latvians viewed themselves as forgotten Europeans whose time as an independent nation in the world community had finally come.

Joseph Stalin felt otherwise. Unable to hold onto the tsar's Baltic provinces during the Bolshevic revolution, he nevertheless coveted Latvia's strategic ice-free ports and growing economic potential. In 1940 he got his wish: Soviet troops occupied Latvia under the pretext of protecting the populace from the Germans. The relentless column of Red Army tanks were followed by a reign of terror that reached all levels of Latvian society. It was then that eleven-year-old Helene Celmina first saw Soviet atrocities against her people. Then in 1941 the Germans invaded Latvia, forcing the Soviets into a hasty retreat. When the basements of the abandoned Cheka buildings were opened, Helene and her relatives gazed in shock at the hundreds of maimed and mutilated bodies of Latvian officers and patriots left by the Soviets. For the young Helene, this sight remained "before my eyes forever."

By 1945 the Germans were defeated and Latvia was occupied once again by the Soviets. In a new wave of terror, thousands of Latvians were deported or executed. The Latvian nation was forcibly annexed to the Soviet Union and the "Russification" of Latvia began.

For Celmina, now a student, the effects of Russification were felt directly and immediately. Her Latvian school texts were replaced by Soviet books which erased all mention of independent Latvia and replaced it with pro-Soviet, Marxist-Leninist propaganda. Like her fellow students, she no longer believed anything she was taught, apart from non-political subjects like algebra or geometry. Even singing classes, which she had always enjoyed, became repugnant, since she was forced to learn Soviet songs.

Celmina now became personally familiar with the dreaded Soviet security forces, known as the KGB in the West and the Cheka in the Soviet Union. Dressed in long leather coats, the Chekists visited her school regularly. One by one the students were summoned to the Cheka offices, questioned, and urged to become informers. Although these interrogations always took place at night, the students were instructed not to tell their parents where they were going or what they were doing. In addition the students were forced to attend demonstrations on

Soviet holidays. Those who refused to participate faced expulsion from school and the deportation of their relatives to Siberia.

In 1947 while living in the Latvian city of Liepaja, Celmina's mother was arrested, charged, and sentenced to seventeen years in prison for "anti-Soviet" agitation. Although this was an abstract, unprovable crime without evidence or eyewitnesses, there was no defense.

Following her mother's imprisonment Celmina traveled to Riga, hoping to move in with her father. On arrival she was refused an apartment permit and was subsequently arrested. Although accused of a long list of cirmes, she received only a one-year prison term. Since she was young and strong, that year was not difficult for Celmina. In fact, she found the experience a valuable lesson in the art of self-preservation in the Soviet system.

At the time Stalin's purges filled the prisons with thousands of political prisoners, mainly peasants and farmers who gave bread to partisans hiding in the forests. Celmina listened intently to prison conversations, familiarized herself with prison routine, and learned much she would be thankful for later.

Following her release from prison, Celmina was understandably discreet and careful. Hope came in 1953 when Stalin died. Although the Russian people cried over the loss of their leader, Celmina, along with the Latvians and other Soviet minorities, breathed with relief: Things were about to change again, but no matter what happened, they couldn't get any worse. Or so they thought.

During the early Khrushchev years, their hope seemed justified. With Khrushchev's "liberalization" many forgot the terror caused by the invidious presence of the Cheka. Latvians began to sing forbidden songs, at first quietly; later, as no arrests were made, their voices grew louder and prouder. Some even related political anecdotes. Tourists arrived in Latvia and spoke with the local citizens in the streets and parks, and in this way Celmina met a foreigner who offered her work as a translator.

At the time Celmina spoke Latvian, Russian, German, English, Swedish, and French. She used her linguistic skills to befriend foreigners, primarily sailors, who supplied her with foreign literature, magazines, newspapers, and books. Like her fellow Latvians, she didn't believe the propaganda of the Soviet press and wanted to hear what the outside world had to say.

Feeling no repercussions for her newfound "education" she wrote to her many foreign friends. Merely receiving letters with foreign postmarks was an indescribable joy. She translated articles from Swedish and Norwegian papers and submitted them to Soviet publications. To her surprise, they were accepted. One magazine, "The Star," published her translation of an article about the animal world.

One day, however, the editor of "The Star" was replaced and "foreign" translations were no longer accepted. Rumors spread throughout the Soviet Union as ministers, editors, and high Communist party officials were suddenly removed from office. The fear that accompanies every Soviet crackdown quickly spread throughout Latvia, as news of arrests, tortures, and imprisonments traveled from city to city. By 1962 talk of massive arrests was everywhere. Helene Celmina was included in this sweep.

One night the Chekists ransacked her apartment and interrogated her. During the search almost all of her possessions were confiscated, including a bag of foreign books in various languages, about fifty magazines, foreign record albums, and all her writing materials. In addition, letters and tape recordings from friends, as well as their phone numbers and addresses, were taken. The search did not stop there. Also taken from her were empty cigarette wrappers (which she had been collecting), a prayer book, an American-made lipstick, some religious buttons, and ink cartridges. An imported chocolate bar and a bottle of whiskey were also confiscated, since according to the Chekists these items were "poisoned" and were sent to the U.S.S.R. in order to kill its citizens.

Celmina was arrested under the charge of "anti-Soviet agitation," an accusation supported by the testimony of an Intourist guide. Celmina had befriended two French tourists, Pierre and Marta Lander, who were members of the French Communist party. In conversation Celmina tried to educate her idealistic friends about what the Communist system had done to Latvia. She told them about the deportations, the Chekist murder squads, the mass executions, and national repression. The

French tourists immediately repeated Celmina's conversations, word for word, to their Intourist guide.

As a result, the Cheka added the additional charge of "spying" and tried to build a case against Celmina. She was interrogated every day for six months at the Riga Cheka. However, when her case finally reached court, the only items used as evidence were sixteen foreign magazines, ten copies of *Reader's Digest*, and several illustrated magazines from West Germany. Everything else taken from her apartment had disappeared, probably into the hands of the Chekists and their families, who were equally hungry for news and products from the West.

Based on this evidence, Celmina was accused of hiding "anti-Soviet materials" with the "intent" of dissemination. Intent was the key accusation, for without it she could not have been charged. Celmina vigorously denied any intent, describing herself as a translator with an interest in foreign languages, explaining that the books and magazines were solely for personal use. Unable, nevertheless, to disprove such a subjective charge as intent, she was found guilty and sentenced to four years imprisonment in a strict corrective labor camp. It is of these four years and the people she met that she tells in *Women in Soviet Prisons.*

After her release in 1966, Celmina spent a futile year-and-a-half searching for an apartment, primarily because no one was willing to associate with an ex-prisoner. However, in 1968 her skill as an artist, accompanied by a stroke of luck, enabled her to win a major Soviet art competition, and with it, a great deal of money.

Her work and acceptance enabled her to save enough money over the next five years to acquire a cooperative apartment, a car, and even a garage. She also met Viktors Kalnins, another ex-prisoner, whom she married. Since they shared common political interests and experiences in the Soviet Gulag, they traveled throughout Latvia, Lithuania, and Estonia visiting and befriending other ex-prisoners. Needless to say, they were continuously watched and followed throughout their travels and were eventually expelled from the Soviet Union for refusing to stop their political activities.

Upon reaching the West, both immediately began a campaign to relate their stories to the free world. They have visited congressmen and senators in Washington, D.C. and members of the Australian parliament. They have lectured and appeared on television in England and Scotland, and continue to travel across the United States and Canada giving interviews and appearing before Latvian émigré groups.

Like many with a stake in the crumbling Soviet system, Lieutenant Kondratovs and Pierre and Marta Lander were unwilling, or incapable, of understanding what Helene Celmina, and others like her, have experienced. Those in the West, far removed from the day-to-day realities of Soviet life, may have difficulty comprehending the society that made such experiences possible. Helene Celmina, however, lived it, and we are all fortunate that she survived to tell about it.

Ojars Kalnins
Chicago
September 4, 1982

AUTHOR'S NOTE

I begin my book with a description of the Riga KGB for two reasons: First, readers familiar with the KGB prison in Moscow may think such a place exists only in Moscow. However, one should open a map of the U.S.S.R. and count the cities in Russia and in all the Soviet republics. In each city there is a KGB prison, known as the Cheka.

The KGB officials are known as Chekists. The term Chekist is not slang, but comes from the acronym of the "All-Russian Extraordinary Commission for Combating Counter-revolution, Speculation, and Sabotage," founded by Lenin and Dzerzhinsky. Each year thousands of Western tourists walk through Dzerzhinsky Square and gaze in awe at the monument and square dedicated to this man. Few realize that Dzerzhinsky was responsible for millions of innocent deaths and that the large building on one side of the square houses the headquarters and main prison of the dreaded Cheka.

As a result the word Chekist is used by the Russians as an epithet, especially when the conversation turns to any evil or unpleasant subject.

The second reason I write about the Riga Cheka is because I became familiar with it after spending six months in a cell for the "crime" of having foreign literature in my apartment.

I want to emphasize that in Moscow and other large Russian cities, the Cheka is not as big a threat as in smaller, non-Russian republics. These provincial Chekists try to please their Russian masters through unlimited loyalty and industriousness in order to gain promotions, awards and medals. As a result, these non-Russian Chekists are overzealous, often arresting and imprisoning untold hundreds of innocent victims. Even if no "anti-Soviet" activity was planned, proof is impossible to establish, for the Cheka can easily claim that the "intent" was there.

All events are true; only a few names have been changed to protect those still alive.

Helene Celmina
September, 1982

WOMEN
IN
SOVIET
PRISONS

CHAPTER 1

INSIDE THE
CHEKA BUILDING

Try as one might, it would be difficult to find a Latvian, Lithuanian, Estonian, or an inhabitant of any of the other "brotherly" Soviet republics unfamiliar with the Cheka. Its name has changed several times: NKVD, MGB, and now KGB, but despite translations into the various national languages of the republics, it is usually called by its Russian initials CHEKA. Cheka is an acronym derived from the initials of the Russian words for "extraordinary commision." The full title of this body, established in December 1917, is the "All-Russian Extraordinary Commission for Combating Counter-revolution, Speculation, and Sabotage." Since this elaborate title might suggest a more respectable institution, the use of the Russian initials eliminates any doubt. The infamous institution, known flippantly as "The Office" among the Chekists themselves, has local nicknames in the Latvian capital of Riga and in other cities and Soviet republics.

One of the oldest names for the Cheka in Riga is "Stabu iela," the former name of the street on which the main entrance is located. After World War II the street was renamed Fr. Engels Street and the nickname changed to the "Corner House." In Liepaja, a port city in Latvia, the Cheka was known as the "Blue Wonder," because it was housed in a bluish-grey building on Toma Street.

It is also safe to assume that no adult in the Soviet Union is ignorant of the functions of the Cheka, or of its great power. Individual Chekists change; some retire, others replace them, occasionally one is fired. Sometimes methods of interrogating, intimidating, and obtaining confessions also change. Only the Cheka itself remains the same. It is, and continues to be, the one institution which can do with people as it pleases. There is no law or paragraph in the constitution which the Cheka cannot alter to suit its purposes.

Also the Cheka is in the unique position of having authority over a number of government departments: the ministry of the interior, the ministry of justice, the ministry of commerce, the port authority, customs, the department of tourism (known as the Intourist), etc. Actually, to describe in detail the activities of the Cheka, or to enumerate its cases and procedures, would produce the world's largest publication, requiring a truck-load of paper. The reader would need strong nerves.

What sort of individual works for the Cheka? Originally, judging from events and known facts, Chekists were hand-picked sadists, often lacking legal training. Later, when Khrush-chev came to power, torture and corporal punishment were forbidden in the Soviet Union. After exposing Stalin's despotism and villainy Krushchev was anxious to avoid negative criticism. Moreover, he wished to appear the opposite of Stalin and to take no more political prisoners. Thus, corporal punishment was officially abolished and political prisoners were renamed "extremely dangerous state criminals."

However, the Cheka continued to work in an altered style. People were arrested and kept in the inner prison of the Cheka. The smiling interrogator questioned, complimented, and occa-sionally, even flattered prisoners. Flattery obtained confessions faster than beatings had; though, frankly, confessions were unnecessary, because people were condemned without them. Nor were sentences lighter. Prison guards and their superiors consider sentences up to five years no penalty at all.

In recent years the educational level of the Chekists has risen considerably. The Cheka selects graduates from law schools who have flawless records and family backgrounds. Such an intelligent Chekist does not feel sympathetic towards another intelligent person who reaches the Cheka as a "crimi-nal." The Chekist will not humiliate and degrade the interrogee, but will talk to the person as an equal, and record everything useful for the writing of the indictment. This method of inter-rogation is dangerous since one reveals his innermost thoughts easily when lured into a friendly conversation.

Everyone in Riga recognizes the Cheka building from the outside. Anyone taken inside once or twice for interrogation

4

remembers little of the interior, having been upset and in no condition to notice. In contrast, those who have "lived" in the Cheka building remember the inside precisely. The entrance to the "Corner House" leads directly into the screening office. Another door connects this small office with the inner rooms and hallways.

The summoned presents his or her notice at the screening office wicket and the attendant telephones the identity inside. The witness is taken upstairs in the elevator to the sixth floor where witnesses, suspects, as well as those already arrested, are "received." Since someone once jumped through the window to his death, the windows have been barred.

A common quip:

Q: "What is the highest building in Riga?"

A: "The Corner House. From the sixth floor, you can see Siberia!"

The Cheka building is laid out in a square, enclosing a quadrangle courtyard. On two sides, at the pavement level, small barred windows face the courtyard. Viewed from the inside, the windows are at the ceiling level. These are the inner isolation cells. Other isolation cells face the other direction where, enclosed by the Cheka building and a high brick wall, lies a small exercise yard, about ten steps below the street and courtyard level. Those taking their walks are unable to see into the isolation cells, as the windows are high when viewed from the little yard.

Deep underground are the showers. When the guard took me down for the first time, I noticed, after descending a whole story undergound, doors on both sides of the dimly lit hallway. Each door had a peep hole and a feeding window. I felt sick because at first I thought that people were imprisoned here. I wondered what kind of prisoners would be confined deep underground. All doors had heavy padlocks, coated with dust. Unnoticed by the guard who was opening the door to the showers, I touched the last padlock with my finger. My touch left a small, dark mark. Later, on every occasion I was taken past these doors, I observed the locks closely, giving special attention to "mine." There was no change. These cells were not used, but were kept in reserve. Nevertheless, in the years immediately after the war, these cells must have been overcrowded, for I heard descriptions of the Cheka's underground cells, in which fifty or more people stood upright day and night because there was no room to sit down.

A trip to the showers came once every ten days. Each time I was issued a small piece of black, foul-smelling laundry soap the size of a matchbox. While I washed, the guard sat in the next room with the door ajar, so she could observe. After the shower, clean sheets were issued and life went on.

Food for those arrested is prepared in the underground kitchen. The kitchen workers are trusted women prisoners, former party members, serving time for petty crimes, such as acceptance of bribes, misuse of position for personal gain, etc. Work in the kitchen is a position of great honor and trust which no other criminal can earn. Good work earns the women good references which open the door to better positions after release. Therefore the kitchen workers are highly motivated and outdo themselves pleasing the Cheka's inner-prison administration.

Food for prisoners in the preliminary interrogation isolation cells was prepared according to definite instructions. This food was incomparably better than that served in general prisons; bread, obtained from the local city bread store, was good. The soups from the Cheka's kitchen contained, apart from lard, potatoes, and other "goodies," large quantities of bay leaves so that the soups were sometimes bitter. Pepper was both expensive and virtually unobtainable on the free market, yet the Cheka used it generously; every bowl contained thirty to forty black peppercorns. Some fished the peppercorns out of their soup, dried and hid them, only to have them confiscated in the next search of their personal belongings. It was forbidden, they were told, to keep pepper in the cells. Who can fathom the Cheka's rules? It seemed, at times, that the guards did not know the rules themselves, or changed them arbitrarily.

Strictest secrecy was observed during the preliminary isolation period to prevent anyone learning who was in the other cells. These cells are not large. The smallest are the single cells which have barely enough room for the bed and the chamber pot—which is not meant only for night use. One cannot walk the length of the bed. On the wall is a shelf to hold a teapot and bread. Spare underclothing must be kept in the bed, either under the pillow or at the foot. To clean the floor, the bed must be lifted and leaned against the wall. There are also cells for two, three, or four occupants. Immediately after their arrest, prisoners are usually assigned a single cell.

The events of an arrest follow a prescibed sequence: Officers arrive at your home, show you the prosecutor's warrant, then ransack your house. You are put into a car and driven to the Cheka's guardroom. Your rings, watch and other personal effects are confiscated. You are thrown into a single cell, the door clangs shut, and you are alone. When a woman is arrested, a uniformed female comes into the cell, orders the prisoner to strip and searches her again. If anything had been missed in the initial search, such as a tiny cross on a chain, it must be surrendered. If the arrested person, for whatever reason, refuses to surrender the cross, she is taken out of the cell to the officer on duty where three men hold her while the fourth removes the cross.

Personal valuables confiscated by the Cheka are never returned. To ensure that the accused know they will never see their belongings again, the clause "with confiscation of property" is added to the verdict in court. This includes all real estate, household goods, and other movable property confiscated at the time of arrest. Anything held in storage for someone else is also seized at the time of arrest; once confiscated, no proof of possession is accepted. Third-party property is also lost.

Should the arrested person protest that he has been imprisoned without grounds, and ask for pen and paper to write a complaint to the procurator, the request is granted. Anyone may write daily to the local authorities of the Republic, as well as to Moscow. These complaints and petitions are carefully read by the interrogator and deposited in some drawer. Rarely is a complaint allowed to reach the outside world.

In the preliminary isolation cells total silence is enforced. Since they can be used for communication, singing and loud talk are forbidden. To summon a prisoner for questioning, a guard opens the food window in the cell door and calls out the first letter of the prisoner's surname. The prisoner must answer, in a whisper, with his full surname. The door is unlocked and the prisoner is led along a green-carpeted hallway to a table holding the register. Entered in this log are the date and time of the prisoner's removal from his cell for interrogation, as well as the time of his return. The prisoner must sign the log under these entries. To prevent his seeing other signatures, a piece of cardboard with a hole large enough for his name is placed over the page at the appropriate spot. The guard holds the cardboard with both hands while the prisoner signs.

Interrogation Procedures

In the interrogator's room, the prisoner sits at his own table. The table is nailed to the floor on the right side, in the corner by the door. The interrogation office door can only be unlocked from inside with a key, although it opens from the outside without a key. This allows other interrogators or their superiors to enter during the process without undue disruption. The windows are barred to prevent any attempts at leaping out. It is virtually impossible to commit suicide at the Cheka.

The questioning procedure is unique. There is reason to believe that actual provable crimes seldom come up before the Cheka, so the interrogator must turn accusation into proven fact. Below are some examples:

Chekist: "You have written to your acquaintances abroad that someone you know has been arrested and sentenced to two years for attempting to cross the border."

Accused: "Yes, I did write that, and what is wrong with it? Two years isn't so long that I couldn't write about it."

Checkist: "How do you know he got a two-year sentence?"

Accused: "His wife told me."

Chekist: "How can you prove that his wife told the truth?"

Accused: "She told me everything in detail; she even cried. And later, when her husband served his sentence, I met him on the street and he told me himself."

Chekist: "That is no proof. They lied."

Accused: "They had no reason to lie to me."

Chekist: "You are proven guilty of spreading false information abroad."

Another case:

Chekist: "During the search of your home, foreign magazines containing anti-Soviet articles were found. These magazines were kept openly where they were accessible to friends who visited you. You insist that you did not keep them for purposes of dissemination, yet anyone could take one and read it."

Accused: "But my friends could not have read them because they don't understand foreign languages. Besides, they haven't shown any interest in them."

Chekist: "How can you say they don't know any foreign languages?"

Accused: "Because I've known them long enough to know that they don't know any foreign languages."

Chekist: "How can you prove that?"

Accused: "If you ask them, they will tell you themselves."

Chekist: "They can say that they don't, but may actually speak several other languages. Can you prove that they don't?"

Accused: "I can swear that they don't, but of course I can't prove it."

Chekist: "Fine, that's all that we need. You can't prove a thing, but you are making a claim."

In this manner, routinely, the guilt of the accused is proved. Each interrogation is an exercise in madness and the Chekist is a madman. It is obvious that the accused has spoken the truth; however, despite the lack of hard evidence, the Chekist must draw up the indictment. Producing facts to substantiate crimes takes time and patience. It is not easy to manufacture crimes where there are none. By law all cases must be completed within two months, but in actuality most investigations drag on for a year or more. Those Chekists who excel in proving non-existent crimes become diplomats. For example Andris Traut-manis, the former Cheka interrogator in Riga, went on to become an ambassador to East Germany.

The Cheka has yet another, although seldom used, method of conducting interrogations: by injection. The drug is probably expensive, or the Cheka would use is more often. In one case, the Cheka in Riga arrested several people on currency charges. This case warranted special attention because the accused used gold. In order to discover the location of the gold, the accused was given an injection. He confessed. Back in his cell, he told his cellmates in total disgust. A few days later the same accused was summoned again. He was a Jew of pensionable age, and the Chekists, suspecting the existence of more gold, gave him another injection. He had nothing left to tell. Back in his cell he complained of illness. Shortly afterwards, he died. His unfin-ished case was marked: "Hearings against Blumenaus discontin-ued, owing to Blumenaus's death."

Let me relate another example of currency crime:

The accused, Gutman, was quite old, and his life story was tragic. He came from Jekabpils, a small provincial town in Lat-via. His family was shot during the German occupation when he was on business in Russia. After the war, he returned to his birthplace to see if anything remained of his father's estate, a house and a jeweler's business in Jekabpils. He went to the father's house, now inhabited by strangers, and found his father's gold hidden in the attic. He remarried, had a daughter, and it seemed that nothing could cast a shadow on the happi-ness of the new family.

Gutman was earning an average salary of eighty rubles a month, about $120.00. Eighty rubles is not enough to live on, no matter how thrifty the family. The child grew; their needs grew. The girl was gifted in music, and since she was studying at the Em. Darzins music academy, she needed a piano.

Several times a year Gutman took one or two gold bars to a

jeweler he knew and asked him to make a bracelet or cigarette case. He paid for the work, but sold the finished article. It never occurred to him that he was committing a crime. He had stolen from no one. The gold was his father's, and since his father was dead, the gold now belonged to him.

Eventually Gutman was betrayed. The interrogator told him to expect severe punishment and confiscation of all property. He knew that he could expect a sentence of fifteen years and had no hope of ever seeing his daughter again; he was already over sixty and under prison conditions fifteen years is a long time. He received permission to write to the director of the music academy, asking for an evaluation of the child's musical ability as well as confirmation of the need for a piano. The director sent a report of the girl's unusual talent, addressed to "the most honorable chairman of the court," with a request to exempt the piano from the confiscation list. In their view the piano was absolutely essential for the girl. As she was only ten years old and had committed no crime, why should she suffer?

The "most humane court in the world" refused the request. Zimins, judge of the Supreme Court of the Latvian Socialist Republic, found Gutman guilty of currency crimes, sentenced him to fifteen years in a corrective labor camp, and confiscated his property.

A prisoner Zbrizher, tried at the same time, was sentenced to seven years of corrective labor and eight years of exile. In preparation for emigration from the Soviet Union, Zbrizher sold everything he owned, including some gold, and bought a sixteen-carat diamond necklace for his wife. Zbrizher's wife testified in court that she thought the necklace was quartz, for which the humane court gave her two years in prison. The diamond necklace was confiscated for the benefit of the state.

Many Soviet citizens do not know even now that surplus gold must be surrendered to the authorities, since it is forbidden to possess or sell even one gold coin. If an old woman takes a five-ruble coin from the days of Tsar Nicholas from her mattress to sell as dental gold, she dares not let anyone know. Otherwise, it means more work for the Cheka, a lengthy sentence for her, and confiscation of her property.

However unbelievable, this is the Soviet reality. It is the same with foreign currency: To buy twenty dollars from a foreigner is a crime punishable by three years in a prison and con-

11

fiscation of all property. On the other hand, gifts of foreign currency from visiting relatives, are permitted. Actually, currency operations are considered criminal offenses, the concern of the militia, the ordinary Soviet police, rather than of the Cheka. However, because the Cheka does not trust the militia, cases relating to currency go through the Cheka. Presumably the Cheka thinks that currency, especially dollars, could be connected with espionage. Any goods from abroad can be interpreted as payment for espionage.

Chekists presume, too, that it is difficult to learn a foreign language, and can be done only with the Party's recommendation, at special educational institutions. Applications for the entrance examinations to Moscow's Institute of Intenational Relations are accepted only from those with a character reference from their local Komsomol committee (Young Communists League), as well as an affidavit from their city's executive committee. The examinations are taken only by those who have approval and a special testimonial from the Cheka.

Any Soviet citizen who tries to learn a foreign language on his own immediately draws the attention of the Cheka which wants to know why he is learning the foreign language. They already consider him a potential spy. If a person fluent in one or more foreign languages meets officials from abroad, diplomats, journalists, or jurists, the Cheka considers him a spy. And if the foreigner gives him a souvenir—a cigarette lighter, a book, or a record album, the act of espionage is proved. The Cheka has only to be informed for the machinery to carry this person to his fate.

Court, Trial, and Sentencing

When the Cheka completes the preliminary investigation, the evidence is presented to the accused in the interrogator's office. The testimony of all the witnesses is included.Witnesses summoned to the Cheka to answer questions about friends and acquaintances require great presence of mind to prevent their testimony from being distorted beyond recognition. If the witness fails to recognize his testimony in court, he is called to the bench and asked: "Is this your signature?" The witness, confused and anxious, is obliged to recognize his signature, but it is too late to protest that his testimony has been twisted.

The next person to be acquainted with the evidence, after the accused, is the procurator. Not every procurator has the right to deal with the cases fabricated by the Cheka, which has its own trusted procurators to deal with these cases.

The trial in court is the final, albeit insignificant, step. It is a mere formality, to which neither the public nor family members are admitted in the cases of especially dangerous state criminals. No one, not even a father or mother can learn on what charges their son or daughter has been convicted. Only when the sentence has been served, should they be fortunate enough to meet again, can the family learn what happened. Often parents die of grief, never knowing what became of their children.

Usually the accused are held in the Cheka's inner prison until the judgment is pronounced. Rare exceptions are prisoners who become ill enough to require hospital care. These are taken to court from the prison hospital. After sentencing prisoners must leave the Cheka. In Riga this meant transfer from the Cheka to the Central Prison, Unit 4, which contained the holding cell for transport prisoners. The next step was to the railway cars. The prisoner transport to the "strict regime" corrective labor camps takes a month. Those convicted of "anti-Soviet propaganda" or "treason against the homeland" are destined for camps with specially chosen guards and strict censorship of letter content. There are no such camps in Latvia.

CHAPTER 2

FIRST ACQUAINTANCES

After several months in solitary, I was suddenly transferred to another cell. The door opened and I stood face to face with another woman. I felt peculiar; after months of no conversation, I was suddenly with another person. I said "Hello."

She responded, "Hello."

After a quick appraisal I was convinced of her rural origin and asked gently, "Do you come from the country?"

She replied energetically, "No, from Moscow."

To give weight to her answer, she struck a pose like an army general reviewing a parade. She told me she studied at the library institute in Moscow, graduated, and moved to Riga. In Riga, however, she was not received with proper respect, given neither a suitable job nor an apartment, and was arrested. Only after recognizing her importance did I have a chance to give my name and to ask for hers, which was Erna.

I looked carefully at Erna again. My first impression was not wrong, she was a country girl. Recalling her complaint about the apartment, I asked, "Where did you live in Riga?"

"With my girlfriend on Moon Street. She used the room, I slept in the kitchen."

"And where was your apartment in Moscow?"

"I had no apartment, I lived in the student dormitory."

"You said you came from Moscow. I thought you were a resident of Moscow," I teased.

She stopped acting so superior. "No, I studied in Moscow for four years."

"Where are your parents?"

"My mother lives in the Latvian district of Tukums; my father is dead, and my mother is remarried."

"But where did you spend your childhood?" I persisted.

"At home with my mother, of course."

"In the district of Tukums?"

"Yes."

"I knew you came from the country," I insisted, because her conceited, aggressive air annoyed me.

"I attended elementary school in the country, but later I went to technical school in Riga."

"All right, all right. Tell the court. I don't need any explanations," I said lightly and began to organize my belongings: a mug, a spoon, a toothbrush and toothpaste, a comb, and a few articles of underwear. We were chatting when I noticed pens and writing paper on her shelf. Surprised, I said, "I see you have a whole office here."

She, in turn, showed surprise. "Why, yes, I need it. I must have paper with me at all times. I can suddenly remember something, and if I do not write it down immediately, I may forget."

"But that is against the rules."

"The interrogator gave it to me, and what the interrogator does is the rule here."

I thought, "Then the interrogator and you, my friend, both sing the same tune."

She had been here since April, I since June. We both started in solitary cells, but she spent only three nights in hers. She was with another woman since. Then the other one was taken away and I was brought in. I could not decide which I preferred: to be alone, or to share a cell with her.

The next day I practically had the cell to myself. Early in the morning Erna was taken upstairs. At noon she was back for an hour, then returned upstairs and stayed until six o'clock. Work usually stopped in the Cheka at that hour, but if the accused or the witness started to say something important, questioning could continue until ten o'clock at night. (Recently night interrogations were discontinued. However during Stalin's regime, most interrogations were held at night.)

Erna was in a good mood upon returning from the interrogation. I thought to myself, this cat likes it here. She told me how handsome the interrogator was, she reminisced about other men, and she bragged about visitors she used to receive at night.

A few days later Erna mentioned that she was involved in a group case with seven men. I was surprised that she had not mentioned it earlier. When I inquired, she insisted that she knew no more.

"How did you get trapped?" I asked.

"I do not know about the others, but I was under surveillance for a long time," she replied.

"How do you know that?"

"Look, I lived on the first floor in a frame house. On the street side the windows were so low that, standing on a stool, any one could see everything that happened in the room."

"You don't believe that the Chekists put a stool to your window and watched what you did?"

"Not always. Only when I had a visitor."

"How do you know?"

"During interrogation they told me in detail everything that had happened in my home."

"You said that you lived in the kitchen."

"They must have looked through the kitchen window."

"I still can't imagine that anyone stood on a stool and watched through the windows."

"They did at my house."

"All right," I said, to finish the futile argument.

Next day, early, a pail of water and a rag were handed into the cell. The previous day, bothered by the dirt on the walls, I asked the guard for soap. The walls were coated with a dark gray oil-based paint. Amused, Erna said I should wash the walls in every cell. When she smiled, her eyes became strangely narrow. Her mouth closed, and her unusually thin lips became even thinner. I finished the walls, washed the floor where my bed stood and passed the pail to Erna.

Then we were taken to the showers. As we passed along the undergound hallway, I noticed that the locks remained covered with a thick coat of dust. In the afternoon we were interrogated upstairs. Erna was taken first. I followed about fifteen minutes later. We went to interrogation daily, as others go to work. Back in the cell I always had the urge to ask how the interrogation went, and relate what happened at mine, but usually I kept most things to myself. Erna returned upset and immediately started to write a complaint to Moscow. It required two days and several sheets. She did not show it to me, but read a few quotes from Lenin. I was amazed and remarked, "You must be a genius to quote Lenin by heart."

"I have read a lot of Lenin. These quotes are not quite by heart. But I know they are from the twentieth volume." She produced the volume. I was speechless, not knowing how to deal with a person who slept on Lenin's volumes in the Cheka.

When I recovered, I asked where she had gotten it.

"I asked for it. There is a library here, and every library must have the works of Lenin."

"You should have quoted Lenin while you were free; now it's probably too late. Or do you plan to gain the favor of some influential person by making him believe your head is full of Lenin and nothing else?"

"Not at all! I use these quotations in my case," came her reply.

I did not want to argue, but I thought: Your case is strange, you are strange, and I do not believe a word you say. I wondered whether she might be a paid informer. I was surprised by her flippant attitude toward her arrest, presence in the Cheka, and expectation of a sentence of no less than seven years.

Her elation upon returning from the interrogation annoyed me, as I always returned depressed. Every question stung like the blow of an invisible whip, leaving a burning pain around my heart for several hours. Inwardly I was always apprehensive; to appear indifferent was exhausting but absolutely necessary when I was shown photographs of acquaintances, because I did not want to talk about them. Therefore, I could not understand how anybody's mood could be improved through interrogation. At those times Erna seemed so unnatural, so exalted that I had no desire to talk to her. Only later did I understand how susceptible Erna was in the proximity of men. Being in the same room and breathing the same air with a man lifted her spirits. However this fact was unhelpful to those men accused with Erna. As she had not seen them for some time, she "neglected" them and did not hesitate to talk about them, saying anything that occured to her, good or bad.

Within the month I was transferred from Erna's cell back to a single cell. I felt like a chess piece which an unseen player moves according to his strategy. Back in the single cell, I did not know whether to be glad or sad. However I was there only one week when the unseen chess player placed me in a cell with an unfortunate woman. Of course, no one told me who she was, where she came from, or why she was here.

When the door opened I saw a well-groomed, well-dressed, deeply distressed woman. In her bright scarlet imported jacket, she sat on the edge of the bed, with tear-swollen eyes. It was clear she came from good circumstances and had led a pampered life. She did not hesitate to tell me what had happened.

Unusual things had begun to happen in Riga. Lawyers, judges, and procurators were arrested. Bribery was involved. Presumably, one could not bribe procurators or judges. Therefore, bribers whose arrested relatives could expect stiff penalties for mismanagement of state property found lawyers who were on friendly terms with procurators. In that manner the lawyers became the middlemen in the bribery cases. The Riga jurist bribery investigation was entrusted to Moscow jurists because, according to law, colleagues in Riga could not be assigned to the cases.

A few days before, my cellmate, a lawyer and middleperson in bribery, was arrested. The arrested jurists had nothing to do with the Cheka, but prosecutors and judges could not be placed in the Central Prison with criminals, because they would be killed within the first few days, without an investigation or judgment. For this reason the Cheka "rented" their premises to ensure the safety of the jurists during the investigation. The lawyers had no reason to fear the prisoners' revenge; they were here for convenience. This woman lawyer had been unable to tolerrate the single cell for more than two days, so she asked her Moscow interrogator to place her with another woman.

In principle everything was clear. Because of her legal training, she was reconciled to her guilt and expected sentence, but she could not deal with the manner of her arrest. It is not enough in the Soviet Union to arrest, jail, and render harsh sentences to innocent people (while many a professional criminal gets the minimum penalty, or even gets off scot-free). The main element of the Soviet system lies in humiliating the arrested person.

If a suspect has taken part in a criminal action, and if he has a permanent residence, nothing is simpler than to go to his home, show him the order for arrest, and take him to jail. The arrest can be made equally successfully in the morning as in the evening after work. If there is doubt whether the suspect is at home, a telephone call can dispel it. But that way there would be no humiliation and the arrest would lose its effect. Therefore, someone decided that my cellmate should be arrested in the courtroom where she was the attorney in a major court case. She was taken directly from the courtroom.

"Three militiamen came in, approached the judge, showed them their documents and told him what they needed" she told me. "Then they came up to me and announced that I was being arrested in the name of the law."

"And you stood up and followed them?"

"Of course. What else could I do? First I picked up my papers, which were immediately taken away from me. I glanced at my clients and they nodded at me for encouragement."

"You had several clients?"

"Yes, four."

"How many were accused in the case?"

"There were sixty people altogether. It was a big case. You may have heard of it, the one about the drivers."

"No, I don't know about it. What kind of drivers were they, why were so many accused?"

"They were bus drivers on long runs. Certain passengers took the buses to work regularly and dropped in their fares, but did not take their tickets. So every day some ticket money got into the drivers' pockets."

"But most people on buses are strangers, except for the morning and evening regulars," I commented.

"Strangers, of course were given tickets. If once in a while someone said that he did not need a ticket, the driver became suspicious and gave the passenger his ticket anyway. Only if some old woman from the country refused her ticket she was not pressured into taking one."

"But how could you defend four clients in one case?"

"If they have no quarrels and contradictions among themselves, it is possible. Besides, they each had their own bus and their own route."

"And it's not enough that they have to go to court. They even have to witness the arrest of their lawyer," I added.

"Yes, that is how those damned officials worked it."

"Would the case have gone on much longer?"

"No, only about two weeks were needed before the sentence."

"Most likely your clients were offered another lawyer?"

"Yes, they were offered one, but all four unanimously declined, saying they did not need another lawyer."

"They must really respect you."

"What respect? What sense is there in talking about respect now that I'm sitting in prison? The drivers counted on me and they declined another lawyer in protest."

I enjoyed the lawyer's company. She had a peculiar name. When she was born in Russia, it was fashionable to give children names relating to the revolution and the party. Spelling "Lenin" backwards created her name "Ninel." Every time Ninel returned from interrogation, her eyes were red from crying, and once inside the cell she continued to cry.

I never cried, and I disliked her perpetual crying, so I tried to divert her. She felt sorry for herself and was anxious for her child who was left in her mother's care. Also she was afraid of losing her husband. The typical Russian scenario goes: As soon as a wife is imprisoned, her husband applies for a divorce to preserve his party honor and his career. Ninel's worries turned out to be well founded. Though the investigation was not completed, it was obvious that she would spend several years in jail. Her husband had already begun divorce proceedings. Despite the fact that Ninel knew our conversations were overheard, she repeatedly advised me how to act at a particular interrogation. Her advice was given indirectly by relating episodes from her practice. She would say, for example: "I have often asked my client 'What devil pulled you by the tail to tell the interrogator things which had not been disclosed and which nobody could prove? By telling the interrogator the whole truth you have created a case against yourself. How am I to defend you? How am I to turn into an unproven fact something you yourself have blurted out?'" Time passed rapidly in Ninel's company because she had many interesting cases to relate.

One day Ninel returned from interrogation visibly upset because two more lawyers were arrested. Unable to control her disgust, Ninel started to rail against the district procurator, a woman, who betrayed everyone. The first one caught was the procurator herself, who accepted a large sum from a mother for her arrested son. In spite of accepting the money, the procurator still requested the maximum penalty for that crime. "Why did she act like that? None of us understand. The only possible explanation is her constant drinking."

"But would she come to court drunk?" I asked.

"Of course she would. I once took part in a trial at which my charming 'procurator' could hardly sit up. She had to support her head with her hand to try to stay awake."

"And you think that she simply didn't realize what she was doing by asking the maximum instead of the minimum penalty?"

"She couldn't have. There's no other explanation."

"What happened next?"

"The mother who paid the money, which she borrowed with great difficulty, shouted and complained through the court that despite her six thousand her son still received the maximum penalty! Let me tell you, that case was unpleasant for the middleman. He's one of my colleagues, a sick man. I feel for him." Ninel continued, "At first the procurator kept quiet and did not betray anyone, as she planned to keep the case from reaching court, since she held such a high opinion of herself and her ability to talk. But when she realized that a trial was unavoidable, she decided that if she had to serve time, so would everyone else."

"Hard-hearted bitch," I exclaimed.

"Hard-hearted, indeed! She lacks a heart altogether. I will never forget the trial at which she asked for the maximum penalty, seven years, for a mother of four small children, for pilfering six spools of thread from the factory after work."

"What did the court do?"

"The court gave her five years, as it had no right to differ by more than two years from the procurator's demand."

"So now, you say, she doesn't want to serve time alone?" I asked.

"Well she asked for the interrogator and listed all the lawyers she could remember, including me. Then she added names of people who had nothing to do with her or the trial."

"So she's dishonest too. Couldn't you sense what kind of person she was before you got mixed up with her?"

"I only had two experiences with her, both for petty hooliganism, involving small sums."

"Now you're in prison because of your kind heart. What sentence do you expect?"

"Up to five years, and after that I will never be permitted to practice my profession ever again. I will only be allowed to work as a law consultant in some factory. My life and my career are finished."

"But what if you moved to another city after you're released?"

"That wouldn't help. In my specialty I couldn't be without a report from my previous job."

"Listening to you I can see mine is the better fate."

"You always compare everything."

"Yes, that comes naturally to me. By comparing myself with another person, I become aware of my own life. When I was put here, for the first few days I thought a gross error had been made, and once it was cleared up, I would be released. When I realized that my release wasn't forthcoming, I became very depressed. But then I thought of Mary Stuart, imprisoned for most of her life, only to be beheaded afterwards. And then my own sorrows, by comparison, seemed so small and unimportant that I had to laugh."

"You are aiming high, comparing yourself to a queen," said Ninel jokingly, "you are a dreamer."

"Queen or no queen, she was a human being, and suffering does not choose its object. Who can forbid me to compare myself to whomever I choose, if that makes me feel better?"

"You're right, it is good to have such a vivid imagination. I see things only realistically and can convince myself of nothing else."

Seeing how much Ninel suffered, I felt sorry for her. We spent a good part of the preliminary investigation time together, before I became seriously ill and was taken to the prison hospital for x-rays. We had grown accustomed to each other and did not want to part. Later I heard via the prison telegraph that Ninel, for her kind heart received the five years. That was a severe penalty. The second, even more severe penalty was the disintegration of her family. The third punishment for the same crime was the loss of the right to continue her practice.

Three severe punishment for one offense: That is the Soviet reality.

CHAPTER 3

THE CENTRAL PRISON IN RIGA

The fate of thousands of Latvians is connected with the largest prison in Latvia, the Central Prison in Riga, which was filled with political prisoners in Stalin's time. Then labor wards, one for men and one for women, each contained between fifty and sixty people. These inmates worked in the prison kitchen, bathing facilities, the hospital, and cleaned the yards and stairwells. Prison II, the former temporary prison was located by the railway station. All four units in the Central Prison were overcrowded with political prisoners, as they were officially called in Stalin's time. They were not trusted with any work within the prison, but sat and waited for their sentence, after which they were sent on the prisoner transport to the "camps of the vast homeland" from the Ural Mountains through Siberia and the far North.

By the time of my arrest in 1962, the whole Central Prison was filled with criminals; there were no vacant beds. Let me describe the prison physically: The windows of the four-story, heavily walled brick building are covered from the outside with what prisoners called "muzzles." These are boards, nailed at an angle over the windows to form skyward slits, the width of three fingers. There is no view down which both prevents the prisoners from seeing through the window, and achieves complete isolation from the outside world. Inside the cell the heavily barred windows are too high to be reached with a hand.

From the outside the prison is secured by three gates: The first gate is open during the day, the second and third which are mechanized are operated by the duty officer. The main entrance of each unit is also secured with a locked, double iron grating. On each floor, both to the left and to the right, are locked grated entrances to hallways leading to prison wards. Behind the door of each ward is another locked iron grating.

The women's wards are locked by female guards, men's by male guards. These guards were both Latvians and Russians, but mostly Russians. It was rumored that one of the Latvian female guards was the prison's executrix of capital punishment. That guard always wore black leather gloves, which were unobtainable in the stores, when she came to lock the doors. It was said that her whole family were prison employees; her husband was a guard of long standing, and her daughter, a young, attractive girl in her twenties, was also a guard.

The floors in the wards and halls are covered with a heavy layer of asphalt, the walls are covered with dark grey, oil-based paint. There are no toilets or water in any of the wards. If anyone becomes thirsty, too bad; if anyone has to use the toilet, there is a barrel in the corner of the ward, which the sixty inmates use day and night. When the barrel is full, two inmates are allowed to carry it out. Quarrels and fights break out because many want to carry the heavy barrel, which often is filled to the brim and spills. Officially there are two trips to the toilet in twenty-four hours, in the morning and at night, between six and six-thirty. It wouldn't be so bad if the human organism could be synchronized with the clock. The so-called toilet is disgusting: four holes in an all-cement floor with no partitions between. Nonetheless the doors of all such toilet rooms are provided with peepholes through which the guards watch. For awhile the toilet paper issued in the Central Prison was a particularly expensive kind: the map of the U.S.S.R. cut into small, four-inch squares. No one ever got two pieces.

The opportunities for washing are practically nil. Lines formed at the four taps, but washing time is limited to one minute per person. It is fortunate that some—the middle-aged Russian derelicts, for example—do not like to wash, and only wet their hands and the area around their eyes. Nothing angers those in line more than an educated Latvian who will not leave the tap until she has washed thoroughly. Fortunately, the water is ice-cold, so that even the most fastidious cannot stand it for long. Also, the washing is interrupted by the insistent rapping of keys against the door, and the guard's clamor that the washing must end, although some have not even had a chance to wet their fingers.

Every ten days my whole ward was taken in single-file to the bathing facilities. There, one pair of nail scissors was issued to every thirty people. When we went to the bath we took our blankets with us to shake the dust out. Sheets were changed then. Underwear was washed in the ward, in a small bowl, all taking turns. The underwear was dried on the end of the bed.

Admitting Procedure

The "order of reception" into the prison is uniform throughout the Soviet Union and follows a strict pattern. Immediately after admission the person is placed in a small closet, called the "box." Often prisoners spend hours, sometimes whole nights, in the stuffy box with only a small piece of netting in the ceiling for ventilation. The box is barred from the outside. This system was adopted to prevent a prisoner from meeting an acquaintance in the anteroom where registration is carried out.

This wait in the box takes place prior to the inevitable search. Everyone brought to the guard room is searched from head to foot. The prisoner is stripped and each garment is searched meticulously. No metal is permitted. If the wedding ring on a fleshier finger cannot be removed, it is filed through and broken off. If a man wears suspenders, these are removed and the pants must be held up by hand. Through all the years of imprisonment the pants must be held up by hand, as the belt, too, is taken away and no cord is allowed. This is also an effective method of preventing escape; running is hampered by the need to hold up one's pants. Neckties and long scarves are confiscated. Pins are removed from a woman's hair. Watches, pencils, mirrors, and all other necessities are removed. Cheap items are thrown into the waste pail, while the valuable ones, as well as money, are entered on a special receipt form. When that receipt is given to the prisoner, he is informed that "these things will be returned to you on release." This is not quite true. The political prisoners have the phrase "with confiscation of all property" added to their sentences, whereas the criminals are informed after their sentence is up that their valuables have been lost.

If the newly arrived woman has been accused of theft, she

is searched internally by a gynecologist. Women accused of other crimes must squat two or three times once they have removed their clothing. Men have their heads shaved, as well as all other body hair. Women have their heads shaved only if lice are found, but their pubic hair is shaved: That added humiliation is mandatory.

When all the "procedures" are finished, the new arrival goes to the stockroom where the following articles are issued: a padded mattress, a dark-colored blanket of questionable cleanliness, two gray bedsheets, a pillow with a gray case, one aluminum bowl, a mug, and a spoon. In many Soviet prisons only the Russian national wooden spoon is permitted, aluminum spoons are not issued. The prisoner must carry these items to the ward. If the prisoner has brought along a bag with personal clothes and underwear, it has to be left in the stockroom for safekeeping. Only the most urgently needed pieces of seasonal clothing are allowed in the ward.

With this newly acquired inventory, the arrested person is admitted to the preliminary investigation ward, which houses many other people who have not yet been tried. The ward sleeps sixty, with bunk beds on either side and a long table and benches in the middle. In the corner is the inevitable reeking barrel. At the end of the table is the tea barrel. Tea is poured twice a day. The rest of the time it is empty. All too often, tortured by thirst, someone tips the barrel sideways hoping for a few drops of cold tea.

The only social diversion in this ward is dominoes. All day long the same players bang the pieces around the table. Others read books. Books are issued every ten days, one to a person, but readers on a ward trade the books they've finished. During the daytime, at the request of the prisoners, the guard allows one or two sewing needles and thread to repair clothes or stockings. There is only a choice between black and white thread. In the evening the needles must be returned.

Handicrafts are strictly forbidden. Nevertheless, occasionally a prisoner will sew or knit something on the sly. Knitting needles are created by peeling the birch twigs from a broom with the spoon. The wool is obtained by unravelling an old woolen garment. In that way old clothes can be turned into new ones. Even though knitters try to work in utmost secrecy, with their backs turned towards the others, they are easy to spot because of the rhythmical movements of their elbows. At least twice a month a major search is conducted. First the prisoners are all lined up, pockets and seams are checked, and then all are led to the exercise yard. On return the knitters find their knitting needles broken and their balls of wool confiscated.

The only officially-sanctioned activity in the preliminary investigation wards is the gluing of gray paper bags which are used by stores for potato packing. For every two hundred bags glued, the prisoner receives a small package of mahorka which is made from stems of the tobacco leaf, cut up fine, resembling sawdust. In Riga mahorka is not available on the free market, but can be found in tobacco kiosks in Moscow and other Russian cities. Newsprint is the only paper strong enough in which to roll a mahorka cigarette. The prisoner must butter up the guards and plead for a sheet of old newspaper in order to enjoy a smoke.

CHAPTER 4

WARD #10

The inmates of the preliminary investigation wards consist of five different groups of people: The main group is comprised of professional criminals, men and women accustomed to the prison rules and traditions since early youth. They are frank, not at all secretive of their past. At times they seem to feel a certain pride in their criminal "profession." The next group is made up of the educated classes representing many professions. Some, the former administrators of various institutions, have accepted bribes. Others are accountants, store managers and other employees with financial responsibilities who were accused of trying to deceive the state for personal gain. Still others are victims of someone else's dishonesty. The third group is comprised of those imprisoned for speculation; the fourth group for vagrancy. And last are the "especially dangerous state criminals," the prisoners who before 1956 were called "political offenders."

According to law the "especially dangerous state criminals" were to be held in solitary confinement rather than be placed with ordinary social offenders. The Central Prison in Riga ignored this regulation. For lack of single cells or for other reasons, the prisoners were mixed in order to house one "especially dangerous state criminal" in each ward.

As previously mentioned, these wards contained people not yet tried or found guilty. But, according to Soviet law, prisoners are guilty from the time of arrest. It is extremely rare for the court to acquit and release a prisoner. These few occurences have been cases of misidentification by a witness. The Russians have a relevant proverb: "If the person was there, the clause can always be found."

One afternoon in November 1962 I was taken to the door of Ward #10 in Riga's Central Prison. A plump, middle aged Russian female guard unlocked the large ward door. I saw before me a typical prison reaction: The eyes of the women inmates froze and their bodies and limbs stiffened. Curiosity alone did not create their degree of immobility. Their stiffness did not pass until the second door, the grating, was unlocked. Stepping over the threshold, I said hello and looked for a place to set my heavy mattress and bedding. When I placed these on the end of the bench by the door, the ward came to life. Half of the women stirred but remained where they were; the rest came toward me to get acquainted. A young woman asked whether I had been brought from the Cheka. Surprised, I asked, "Where do you know me from?"

"I have heard a lot about you," was the answer.

Local news travels much faster in prison than in the outside world. I asked her, "What case are you involved in?"

"I am here in the Jesus case," was the proud reply. "You have probably heard about Jesus," she added with a smile.

"I have heard abut him, but have never met him. What about Jesus?" I asked, sensing bad news.

"He is here in prison. I am accused as a collaborator, and soon we will have a trial."

"He's in prison? Ten years ago Jesus was threatened with prison, but he entered the insane asylum."

"Yes. He simulated insanity and came out scot-free, but this time he was arrested because the evidence was so strong."

I remembered visiting Jesus in the mental hospital years earlier. My relative who accompanied me explained that after the war many people lacked documents. Those with money and connections bought papers from Jesus. Through these documents, which he produced with his own hands, he saved many people from inevitable inprisonment and deportation.

These people went on to live and work normal lives. Hence the nickname, Jesus. Although Jesus was extremely helpful, some-one betrayed him and he was arrested. With his sharp mind, he decided to simulate insanity. My relative, for whom Jesus produced a high school diploma, visited him in the hospital from time to time. This diploma enabled my relative to avoid losing two precious years and start university immediately.

"And he had no chance of avoiding prison this time?" I asked.

"No, none at all. During the ransacking of his home, the militiamen found a notebook containing the names of his clients and the documents issued. The notebook, hidden behind the stove, provided such damaging evidence that nothing could be done."

"And how are you involved?"

"I was the contact person for a few customers, some of whom needed sick-notes to verify absenteeism from work."

"I see, and if such a notebook exists, everybody can be found for whom documents were produced."

"Yes. Ironically, lots of his clients are jurists, prosecutors, and investigators who received their university diplomas from Jesus."

"Oh my, what's going to happen to them?"

"Who knows? Actually, they should be fired, but many of them are highly regarded members of the Party and have worked as investigators for years."

"I suppose he can expect a long sentence" I said gloomily.

"Yes, no less than seven years, but possibly ten."

Helene Celmina

"What about you?"

"My investigator told me to count on a couple of years."

It is typical of the Soviet investigation process that the investigators know in advance the judgment of the court. This case was no exception. As I learned later, Jesus received eight years in a corrective labor camp, and my conversationalist, two years. Their only advantage was that they were not sent away as are political prisoners, but remained in Latvian territory.

Since I had gained a friend, I was no longer among strangers. It is comforting in prison to have a friend. After our exchange she went to the cupboard and returned with a slice of bread and fat for which I was grateful; but I wondered about her "luxurious" living.

"Did the investigator allow you to receive parcels from home?" I asked.

"What do you mean, allow? We all receive what the law allows: not more than one parcel in two months."

I explained that in the Cheka my investigator ignored the laws, so I received nothing. This aroused the indignation of nearly every inmate.

I thanked her for the sandwich. It was more than half a year since I tasted anything that good. My bed was the upper bunk, third from the door. I was overjoyed that it was not next to the barrel. My neighbor in the other bunk was a young pleasant looking girl with a complicated case. After graduating from a technical school, she worked as an animal technician on a kolkhoz (collective farm). Lightning killed a bull, and she sold the meat at a reduced price to an establishment that raised fur animals. The small animals, mink and nutria, ate the meat and died. The silver foxes became sick, but survived. Because this was not a standard case, determination of the length of the sentence was left to the discretion of the court.

When I voiced my amazement, an animal technician from another kolkhoz came over, claiming that her case was still graver.

"What did you manage to do?" I asked.

"Yes, 'managed to do' is right. We had a contract to deliver a certain number of bull calves for breeding to Central Asia. A couple of calves were born with a small white spot on the forehead. Because purebred cattle are dark brown, a white spot is not acceptable. I dyed the white marks on two calves with hair dye. After the calves had been away for a few months, the color must have washed out or faded. Someone noticed the white marks. Now I will have to answer in court."

Listening to such an extraordinary story, I almost burst out laughing. The irony was too much: A pretty, young country girl, by using her peasant cunning, became a dangerous criminal. She waited a long time for her trial, and I never heard what her sentence was.

The appearance and behavior of another prisoner suggested she had received a good education. She obviously spent much of her life in better society. Her hair was completely white, although she was barely sixty years old. Everyone addressed her respectfully as "Mrs." Despite the surface appearance of a spoiled, fine lady, she bore her fate heroically: She did not despair, and hardly ever cried. When I inquired what she was accused of, the answer was lengthy.

"All of us at the silk department of the Army Economy Store were arrested. We, the cashiers, received the money and gave part of it to the manager. She, in turn, gave part of it to the director, who paid dues to the director of commerce. I was only a small link in the chain and hopefully will not receive many years."

"And is the whole department in prison?"

"Yes, in various wards, throughout the prison. There are about thirty people."

"Couldn't they have left people like you at home until the trial? You wouldn't have fled anywhere, would you?" I asked.

"Never. I have asked to return home until the trial. Yesterday I sent my latest appeal to the procurator of the republic, explaining that I have a severely retarded twenty-three year old daughter with the mentality of a three year old. Someone must be with her at all times. My other daughter is only seventeen. She has to finish school and it is difficult for her to study and manage everything."

"And they haven't seen fit to release you despite such extraordinary circumstances?"

"No. I have appealed in writing six times already, but it is like talking to a brick wall. On account of my sick child I could never run anywhere."

Every day this pleasant lady hoped that she would receive permission to leave the prison at least until the trial. Days passed and nothing changed because procurators are not interested in patients or children at home. They go strictly by the state laws which say criminals belong in prison.

In the evening of my second day I noticed that the long table in the center of the room divided in half not only the number of beds, thirty in each half, but also the categories of prisoners. On the right, where I had my bed, was the so-called "fine society," whereas those on the left were almost all Russians, including prostitutes of all ages. The young Russians formed one group, the old ones another. The young were arrested mainly for petty larceny, the old ones for vagrancy, as well as larceny. The young ones found prison life rather romantic; in thoughtless levity, they often sang and acted merrily. Occasionally those with the loudest voices were put into the punishment cell, which gave them something to boast about to the young male thieves.

Russian prisoners often have no relatives. The older ones simply do not know what has become of their relatives: They were, for the most part, heavy drinkers, and had not kept up with family. The young ones, as a rule, with few exceptions, came from orphanages.

From long wear, the elbows of my knitted sweater were giving way. Everyone who sits in prison knows what to do

Ward 10

when that happens: The sweater must be unravelled, wound into balls of wool, the balls hidden, and a new sweater knitted on the sly. This project has two advantages: One is the outcome, a new sweater; the other is an occupation, something to do, so the days go faster. It is common for a prisoner to approach a knitter about the pattern of the garment. One day a middle-aged Russian, bored and lonely, sat down beside me and asked "What is the nice thing you are making?"

"A new sweater. What else?"

"Yes, you Latvians know how to do everything."

"But who prevents you from learning?"

"You will never understand. You live a different, valuable life. It is not the custom with us Russians; we have much to learn from the West."

"What do you mean?" I asked cautiously. She sighed, and was silent. Then there was a sudden glimmer in her eyes, like a little devil stirring.

"Do you have any idea who I am?"

"I think you are, for the time being, an unfortunate like the rest of us."

"This is the fifth time I have been in prison."

"Really? I thought everyone here was a first offender, with the repeaters in the other ward."

"I am only telling you; you always tell the investigator it's your first offense, so the punishment is lighter. If the trial is held each time in a different republic, they usually can't trace the previous arrests. Besides, thieves never carry documents and, when we're arrested, we make up new names and birthplaces, usually choosing cities which suffered most during the war because their registry offices have been destroyed."

The Russian woman went to her bed and returned with cigarettes and matches. The thieves had everything. She offered me a cigarette and we smoked while she continued, "Some people in our category actually don't know their real name or birthdate."

"How is that possible?" I asked.

"The majority of people in our category come from orphanges, myself included. At the end of the war there were so many homeless children in Russia. The older ones stayed in hiding to prevent being captured and placed into orphanges, which were merely prisons. Some more fortunate were taken in by strangers. The unclaimed foundlings were given new names in the orphange."

"Do you know anything about yourself?"

"I remember a little. I was seven when the war ended. I came from Leningrad. My mother was a physician at the front, my father an army officer. Neither returned. My grandmother died of hunger during the blockade. She probably gave what little food there was to me and went hungry until she died."

"You must have had an apartment in Leningrad with furniture and other possessions."

"I suppose so, but I don't remember. When my grandmother died I didn't understand; I thought she was sleeping. I don't know how many days I slept in bed with my dead grandmother. I only remember being weak from hunger. Our neighbors shook their heads and said that my grandmother had been dead for several days. Then I was placed in an orphanage. *C'est la vie.*"

"Do you speak French, too?"

"I remember a few words. My grandmother was a French teacher before the war. In her youth she had lived in Paris."

"I suppose you had school in the orphanage."

"There was a school, but we didn't learn much because the teachers were sent to the front to act as medical nurses. Our teachers were uneducated old women. They taught us to read and write a little, that was all."

"Why do so many professional thieves come from the orphanages?"

"We saw nothing but theft in the orphanage. Beginning with the director and ending with the cook and kitchen staff, they stole everything that was meant for us. The children were always hungry. We never had enough to eat because the small amounts the state allotted us were stolen by our so-called teachers for their own children. When we were hungry and couldn't sleep, we tiptoed out to watch the flour and groats that had been delivered to the orphanage during the day packaged and carried away at night. That's where we learned to steal. It was a school for thieves. Professional thieves who grew up in orphanages live by the motto: 'They stole, we steal.'"

"I can understand how you learned to steal and why. But you keep getting caught and imprisoned. Don't you have any desire to start a family and work and live a normal life?"

"Of course. But to establish a family you must live and work somewhere. But no one wants to register or employ orphans. Besides, you need help. Without relatives or friends to help, one's whole life is spent in prisons."

"How did you get to Riga and where did you stay?"

"On the train, of course. I stayed in Kengarags with a girl I know from the prison in Leningrad. Later she was imprisoned in Riga for theft. She is young and pretty.

After release, she married a sailor. An apartment was assigned to them. I came for a month of 'guest performances' in stealing, but got caught."

"One more question. What is your specialty, pockets or apartments?"

"Pockets. For apartments you need help. One person can't manage alone."

Our cigarettes were finished and so was our conversation. I concluded that this twenty-six year old woman, who I first thought to be at least ten years older, was tired of sitting in prisons. The thoughtless years of her youth were over and she had come to Riga to search for a man and an apartment. But since she continued to support herself through theft her past repeated itself. However for her immediate future, a life in Riga was guaranteed. She would serve her time, two or three years at most. The female camp is located on the south side of the river on Daugavgrivas Street, where the ordinary criminal offenders are taught to sew men's shirts for stores in Riga. When half of the term has been served, a special parole commission cuts the sentence in half for good behavior and good work.

Then she would receive the money she earned and a diploma for completing the sewing course given in the corrective labor camp. She would also get a good character reference entitling her to work in any sewing factory in Riga and a place in the communal home. Ironically through her theft she will be granted entrance to a good life. In a year she will speak from the platform, saying "Thank you, great Communist party and government," and Riga will have been enriched by yet another loyal daughter of mighty Russia.

Riga is being filled with these models of loyalty. Today, no thief who has been caught in Riga and served a sentence within Latvia is sent back to Russia. They all have the right to employment in a factory or in construction, and to live in communal homes. After a few years, if not caught and returned to prison, they are assigned an apartment.

After this conversation I was troubled and could not sleep. The frank story of this Russian woman reminded me of the extensive privileges the Russians have in our country. As I was tossing and turning, incidents I had observed in the stores, central market, and streetcars of Riga flashed through my mind. I witnessed Russian teenagers picking Latvians' pockets. When they saw me watching, one showed that his hand, wrapped in a dirty rag, held a razor blade. When a razor blade is shown, you must turn your head immediately. Otherwise, they will cut a cross on your face with the razor blade, saying, "You saw, you won't see anymore."

I remembered the times I was victimized by pickpockets. My first salary was taken on a sunny summer day. I bought ice cream by the cinema only to discover about five minutes later that my money was gone. Another time, in the market place, I put my purse in front of me. While I was sampling butter, the purse vanished. Again, on another occasion, in the summer of 1948, I needed some money, so I sold some coat material I had purchased before the war. Having carefully deposited the money in my purse, I bought a few items for dinner at the market place. Then someone mentioned that my handbag was open. The money was gone. I cursed the thieves who came like swarms of locusts from Russia to the Baltic republics for their so-called "guest performances!"

Now, I was sitting in the same cell with one of them, in equal circumstances, but with unequal rights. She would get a shorter sentence than I. She would be under the ordinary regime, I under the severe one. She would serve her sentence in Riga, I would be sent on prisoner transport to Russia. Her sentence would be cut in half, mine would not. She would be eligible for amnesty, I would never be eligible for amnesty. And truly, who was the worse criminal when our life stories were compared: She had four imprisonments behind her, not including the thefts for which she was not caught. Consider how many people suffered as the result of her activities, how many tears were shed, how many people faced grim circumstances. In contrast, for reading foreign books and magazines in my own home, I would be given a sentence at least twice as long and twice as severe. No, there is not and will never be justice in this land.

These thoughts plagued and oppressed me all night until morning, when it was my turn to carry out the full barrel. My partner was stronger and pulled ahead. With every unmatched step the nightly brew of sixty women splashed onto my feet and the hallway floor. When we arrived at our destination, both feet were thoroughly wet and stinking. As we tipped the barrel, my soaked feet received an additional splash. Then we had to take the birch twig broom, dip it into the chlorine, scour the inside of the barrel, rinse it, and carry it back. I gave my feet the same scouring treatment.

Distributing sugar was the next compulsory task for the person on duty. The ward received one bag of sugar: Each person was entitled to one tablespoon which had to last for twenty-four hours. Usually the sugar was poured on the bread ration. Some held out their mugs for it.

The next task was carrying the tea-barrel in from the hallway and lifting it onto the table. The aluminum barrel was always so hot that it could not be handled without a towel. After breakfast everyone stood in line in pairs to be counted. The supervisor entered and was given the number of people on the ward. Then came the daily washing of the black, asphalt floor. (The asphalt on highways is a much higher quality than that on the floors in Riga's Central Prison.)

Events in another woman's preliminary investigation affected our ward. When anything unusual happens in a prison or in a corrective labor camp, all inmates must present themselves to the superior. If the administration cannot find the guilty party, at least they discover who has been friends with whom, and the friendships that have angered the camp or prison officials are mercilessly torn apart. One of these "suspicious" friends was reassigned to our ward. She could not go unnoticed.

At first glance she appeared pretty, although she lost her hair, apparently in a struggle with prison guards. These struggles usually end with the prisoner in the punishment cell. If she continues to vent her emotions she may be taken to the barber's where neither vows nor pleadings help. This young woman had obviously been to the prison barber recently.

When she opened her mouth to tell us which ward she came from, I froze. She was no more than twenty or twenty-five, but there was not one whole tooth in her mouth. Some were missing altogether, others resembled ruins of old castles with a mixture of darker and lighter spots. When she had everybody's attention, she removed her knitted sweater to reveal her sleeveless shirt. Both arms up the shoulders were covered with tatoos. We no longer needed a newspaper; we could read her like a kiosk. However, most of the text referred to sex and was too vulgar to be interesting.

When she felt sufficiently admired, she sat down elegantly and told us her story. Four women who met on the ward became good friends. They sent ardent love notes through the window to the men below, vowing to belong to them at the first opportunity. Although the lovers had never seen one another, a self-portrait in a few short words on an empty cigarette carton, written with matches wetted with saliva, whetted interest. Eventually when promises were no longer enough, the young women showed more initiative than could be imagined. From a bed they removed a piece of iron by bending it back and forth. In the darkest corner of the ward under a bed, they scraped the floor with this piece of iron all day long until there was a hole in the asphalt. They gradually crumbled the reinforced concrete under the asphalt by working shifts from morning till night. They carefully hid the broken pieces of concrete under their clothes and in pockets, to be discarded on their walks outside.

They worked on the floor for about two weeks to make a hole wide enough to crawl through. The floor was so thick that only when one lay down with her shoulder on the floor could she reach the bottom of the hole with her hand. At that depth the first tiny opening to the men's ward appeared. The hardest part was removing the remaining thin layer in order to reach the men. However with bliss so near, a man who had nothing to do with the love affairs showed the guard what was happening. From then on there was nothing but trouble. When the whole ward, one by one, was interrogated in the superior's office, no one breathed a word. No one knew anything. A ward without an informer is a rarity. The officials admitted that this was a first in the history of Riga's Central Prison. In great admiration they measured the width and depth of the hole.

I experienced another surprise when a prisoner, a Latvian who kept to herself and read books, asked me if I attended a certain school in 1939. Only rarely does one recognize a schoolmate after twenty-three years, and it is rare to meet in a prison ward. When we reminisced, she remembered everything about me, while I remembered nothing of her. Usually the younger children notice and remember the older ones, this time the older one remembered the younger one. She was three grades ahead of me at the time, but noticed me because of my braids. No girl in the school had braids as long as mine. Lita told me about herself.

"Maybe you remember our house with the large garden around it, even if you do not remember me."

"I remember your house well; it was the most beautiful one in the district."

"It was taken away from us and my parents were sent to Siberia. At the time, I was visiting relatives in Liepaja, so I was not taken and nobody looked for me."

"Who is in your house now?"

"It is now an old-folks home and something like a mental hospital."

"Where did you live then?"

"Of course I never returned there. I married and lived in Riga."

"Why are you here now?" I asked, after a short silence.

"You see, in life it so happens that some people steal and others have to answer for it. I was the manager of the milk department in the grocery store on the corner of Lenin Street."

"What kind of penalty are they planning for you?"

"It's hard to tell. Perhaps some accounting error will be found which would be in my favor, as I can simply not understand how such enormous amounts can be missing from milk products, which are the cheapest."

"Then it is a case of large amounts?"

"Yes, at the present some seven thousand rubles are mentioned."

We continued talking about old times and mutual acquaintances. Finally, we both admitted no one can escape fate, everyone must suffer, and everyone has to spend some time in prison, regardless of social, financial, and educational standing.

I felt sorry for Lita, who suffered greatly from the circumstances, like so many other Latvian women. In addition, she frequently suffered heart spasms of several minutes. On these occasions a doctor on our ward rushed to insert a spoon between her teeth to prevent her from accidently biting her tongue. No help came from the prison medical staff. No one paid attention to Lita's complaints about her poor health. She was only given a few nitroglycerine tablets to take when the spasms started.

According to law, the prison hospital is only for those who become sick while in prison and for maternity cases. The law makes no exceptions for pregnancy, which is not considered at the time of arrest. On the ward there was a Latvian woman who was the bookkeeper for a kolkhoz. Because of a large deficit found in the operation, the bookkeeper was imprisoned in her sixth month of pregnancy. I heard later that her child was born in prison, while her mother received fifteen years in a correction camp. In cases like this the child is placed in an orphanage. When her sentence has been served, the mother reclaims her child.

The doctor on our ward also expected a stiff sentence. She was a gynecologist, and unable to exist on her salary, she supplemented her income by performing abortions. She had already been on trial once, this was her second time. This gray-haired doctor, about sixty, bore her fate courageously, although her penalty would be greater this time. The court emphasizes specifically that, if the person has not improved after the first penalty, the second punishment must be more severe. The court never considers that a physician cannot exist on her salary. Since abortions are legal in the Soviet Union, a practicing physician would be punished only in rare cases where the patient died. Then the physician could be tried for manslaughter. The physician on our ward was to be tried for doing the abortion for a profit. It is worse for abortionists without medical training. They are tried both for performing the abortion and taking money for it.

Our ward held several former Party "ladies," no longer Party members because it is not permitted to imprison and bring to court Party members. Those who must be imprisoned are first expelled from the Party. One of these had held a high position as the chairman of the Soviet executive committee in a Latvian town. She received a sizeable bribe from a wealthy man to whom she had granted materials for a slate roof.

Despite their expulsion from the Party and their presence in the ward, these women remained apart, associating with no one from the other groups. Nothing could dampen their feelings of superiority, acquired while holding responsible party positions. They viewed every one of us with contempt.

The women caught and imprisoned on the speculation clause were amiable, helpful, and good natured. It was unfortunate that they could expect comparatively high penalties. In Latvia, mostly Latvians are imprisoned for speculation, sometimes an odd Jew or Gypsy, but rarely a Russian. One can speculate with anything that cannot be obtained in the stores. One of these women expected a stiff penalty because hers was not a simple speculation case. She and her sister bought wool, knitted sweaters with knitting machines, and sold the finished product. Speculation plus home industry, is a grave crime according to Soviet law.

To prevent the sisters from collaborating on their testimony, they were separated, and each placed in a different ward. They were interrogated separately and their testimony compared. The interrogation continued until there were discrepancies. However, because they were taken to court together, they would be allowed to suffer the penalty in the corrective labor camp together.

An unusual case involved an old country woman imprisoned for giving a bribe. The bribe was small, only one hundred rubles, and probably she received no more than a year in prison. In her simplicity the old woman did not know how to present the bribe properly. Therefore, the official receiving the bribe delivered the old woman to the militia.

Two Latvians were imprisoned for theft. It is important to distinguish between "a theft" and "thieving." "Thieving" refers to the systematic activity of acquiring somebody else's belongings, just as a "thief" designates a profession. Neither of the two Latvians could be categorized with the "thieves." Rita, the younger, eighteen years old, was naive, always smiling, with kind eyes. At floor washing time she always helped lift the benches onto the table. A pleasant, amiable youngster, she visited her grandmother who sent her to the attic to take the washing off the line. Rita continued, "I knew which lines held my grandmother's washing. I knew and recognized the other clothes which suddenly seemed so desireable." Rita blushed and continued, "I thought nobody would find out. I took a blouse. I reached the door and then noticed a skirt, too, a checkered one. Again I couldn't resist. I took the skirt, as well as a lace slip."

"Where did you intend to sell the clothes?" asked an older woman. Rita blushed deep red.

"I wanted to wear them myself. I did not want to sell anything," she said.

"And perhaps visit grandmother," another voice added maliciously.

"No, I would not have worn them to grandmother's. I wanted to wear them to a dance and return them afterwards."

"And what about it, did you delay it too long?" still another woman joined the conversation.

"I couldn't so . . . all at once," Rita became confused, as she would have at the interrogator's.

I joined in, "Maybe it was hard for Rita to give up the beautiful clothes if they looked good on her and she still wanted to enjoy them longer."

"Yes," Rita responded with relief.

"To pay for that with two years is not worth it," added the older woman.

"It depends how you look at it," thought another one.

Later we heard that because Rita came from a poor family, could not afford good clothes, and had frankly confessed, the court gave her only one year in prison. In contrast, I do not know the outcome of the other much graver case, involving theft from the state. A man and a woman were imprisoned, a sign that the case was comparatively serious. Three people were present at the scene of the crime, but, according to witnesses, only two committed the theft.

One summer morning three people in a jovial mood left a party. They were ordinary working class people without titles or academic degrees. It was Saturday morning, and they did not have to report for work in the factory. Humming, they walked along the streets of Old Riga, arriving at a grocery store where cases of milk and cream were stacked because the store was not yet open. Because their thirst was intense, the man removed three bottles of yogurt drink from the upper case and handed a bottle to each. The woman grabbed a jar of cream which she thrust into her purse. They "forgot" to leave the money for their "purchases."

They did not get far from the scene of their crime, for the alert eye of the nation does not sleep even in the early morning. The militia received a telephone call that grocery store #71 had been robbed. All three were arrested, but the one who had not taken the yogurt drink, only consumed it, was released. The total amount of the robbery came to a total of one ruble and thirty kopeks. For one ruble and thirty kopeks, two people sat in prison. Because the court deals with the cases in the order they occur, the two already waited several months for their turn in court. It would be more profitable to the state not to send these people to prison. Let them pay the one ruble, thirty kopek deficit and continue their work.

A little more about prison life and minimal conveniences should be mentioned.

Food was provided three times a day: Breakfast was bread, hot tea, fifteen grams of sugar, and salted fish. Dinner was cabbage soup and barley porridge. For supper we had soup in which a fish had swum.

Amusements were determined by the prisoners' age and category. The main diversion for the thief category, both women and men, is angling, whereby a "fishing line"' is dropped through the window from one floor to the next to pass messages, cigarettes, etc. The second most popular diversion is the opportunity to wash stairwells and hallways. Again the monopoly belonged to the thief category. Since all wanted the opportunity and only four were taken at a time, frequent fights resulted.

The greatest diversion for the intelligentsia with personal money in the prison cashbox was the bi-monthly visit to the prison store. Working the night in the kitchen was the second best diversion. Washing the large porridge kettles, on the bottom of which something edible might be found, was done by the stronger women. Those with less strength peeled potatoes and ate one or two. In all U.S.S.R. prisons only male thieves are trusted with food preparation.

A woman specially selected from the ward cleaned the prison director's office. This task was not entrusted indiscriminately, as large amount of writing supplies and other objects could disappear if a thief did the cleaning. As one of the last diversions, emptying the barrel should also be mentioned.

The rest of the time everyone remained in a sitting position. Sleeping is allowed only by special permission from the doctor. Generally, according to the rules the inmates must sit at the table from six in the morning till ten at night, but this rule was not strictly enforced. Sitting on the bed was not prohibited. However, if someone sitting on the bed fell asleep, the alert eye of the guard noticed. The guard pounded on the door and woke the inmate, threatening that sleeping during the day could earn her the punishment cell. During the night it was mandatory to sleep in such a position the the guards could see one's head.

One day my turn came to visit the prison x-ray office. After the scan, while still in the darkened room, I was told that I had two ulcers, one in the stomach and the other in the duodenum. I would be placed in the hospital for treatment. The Russian doctor asked me what I was accused of. When I answered she shook her head but said nothing.

CHAPTER 5

THE PRISON HOSPITAL

The next morning, after breakfast, I was told to return all equipment, including the mattress and bed linen. I took them to the basement where I had received them. Then, with my hands behind my back, I was taken across the yard to the incomparably cleaner hospital block, to a small room with two beds. I was amazed at the luxury of a room with only two beds. One bed, opposite the door, was occupied; the other, at the left along the wall with the head opposite the door, was visible through the spy hole. Each bed had a cupboard. The first bed was occupied by an elderly woman of indeterminable nationality. I said hello, and she answered in Latvian. We exchanged names. If ever anyone's name was completely incompatible with her personality, it was that of Maiga Laimina (gentle bringer of luck).

Maiga had coarse features: Her lean and bony face was more like that of a man than of a woman; her eyes lay deep in the hollows. Her voice was deep and hoarse as if from chronic drinking. She was weak and spent her time lying in bed. We talked about her illnesses. The fact that she had cancer in the last stages suprised me because it is customary to conceal such facts from the patient. Finally I asked, "Have you spent a long time in the hospital?"

"In two days it will be three months," was the reply.

"And in prison altogether?"

"Two years and four months."

"Is your investigation taking that long?"

"Not at all. I was sentenced long ago and spent one and a half years in the camp. Then the camp doctors refused to treat me and I was brought here."

Her reply made me cautious; I sensed something not quite right with this woman. I knew prison laws. The unsentenced were never placed with the sentenced. If she had been sentenced and I was placed with her, she must be an informer or, in prison slang, a "broody hen." I decided to be on my guard.

"How many years did they give you altogether?"

"Five years, but I will not finish them. I'll die here."

That day she seemed sick and we did not talk much. Plagued by curiosity, I asked her what she was sentenced for.

"For fraud," she answered, as if she were joking. "I received money from several people, for whom I promised to obtain deficit merchandise. I had connections in several stores, where I could get the merchandise, but they did not have the goods immediately. Later during a large drinking bash this money was used to buy drinks. What can I do? I was a stupid old bag, a weak character, now I have to squat in the slammer."

"Did you leave a family at home?" I asked in a compassionate voice.

"Of course, my old man was left alone, my son married last year."

"All of you couldn't come up with the money and return it?"

"How do you get what is not there? No use asking my son, who is too proud. And he would not have had that much either. He plays the fine fellow, eats in restaurants.

We have never gone to restaurants, we are satisfied at home."

The next day my suspicion was confirmed. After breakfast when the medicine was distributed and no one disturbed us, Maiga suddenly started to question me about people I knew. "I know a certain Nina, I once bought an imported jacket from her, don't you know her too?"

"Yes I do, so what?" But Maiga asked several times, then seemed to share what she knew, and then asked questions again. Maiga's assignment was obvious. When it appeared that I knew Nina no more than Maiga, she asked about another. After a few days she tried to take up the conversation about the same acquaintances, and when nothing resulted, we chatted casually.

Then one day Maiga was called to "the doctor." The regular doctor's visit came every morning after breakfast. I was never called out of the ward to the doctor. I must have been considered an idiot for such an obvious attempt to be made on me with the "broody hen," Maiga. When Maiga returned in a couple of hours from the "doctor," she carried a parcel. "Imagine what a joy! My old man brought me a parcel. Already at the door, I was called back to sign for a parcel from the old man." In a coquettish way she added, "The old devil remembered his old woman after all!"

That she was glad about the parcel, I understood. And that the parcel was not from her old man I understood too as soon as she started to arrange the items on her cupboard. There were about ten packages of cigarettes, gray bread from the prison store along with the prison store margarine, melted cheese and cookies.These items were wrapped exactly the same as those bought in the prison store by the women who had money in the prison cash-box. I pretended ignorance. Later I thought I should have told her to her face: I know where this comes from. At that time, I held my peace and said nothing, not wanting to make an enemy. We had to live together in the same room. Besides, Maiga was not stingy; she immediately gave me a package of cigarettes. I wanted to smoke and there was little left of the mahorka the elderly prostitutes in ward #10 rolled for me.

That day she left me alone, probably on the "doctor's" instructions. Nevertheless the next day she resumed questioning, asking about people I knew and whom she could not have known. It became clear that she did not know the "mutual" acquaintances discussed on previous days either. Her hollow conversations continued for about two weeks. Neither was I the worse for them, nor did she profit. Finally I was informed that my trial would start in four days. Worried, I could neither sleep nor eat.

I went to court every morning, as others go to work, and returned in the evening. After three days the head of the guards refused to drive me to court because my vomiting soiled his automobile twice a day and there was nobody to clean it. I had never had motion sickness before. In the morning when I stepped into the barred cage, I was fine, but as soon as the vehicle started to move I felt terrible and in ten minutes I was sick. The intense vomiting exhausted my strength so that when we arrived at the courthouse I could not climb out of the vehicle without the soldier's help. After drinking cold water I felt better. Once I lost consciousness in the courtroom. The ambulance came from the hospital and I was given an injection. The court recessed. When I felt better, proceedings continued.

In the evening, as I stepped into the vehicle, I felt fine, but as soon as we were in motion, I became sick. To prevent a mess, I was lavishly "fed" with medication in the morning, with more taken along for later. The most trying time came in the evening, when I was taken into the large prison hall and placed in the cupboard. There were about twenty cupboards, one person in each, to prevent people from seeing one another. From the cupboard the prisoners went, one at a time, behind a curtain to strip for the personal search. Only then were the prisoners returned, one at a time, to their wards. One often squatted in the cupboard for hours, awaiting return to the ward. One evening on returning from the court, I found a strange woman in my bed. To my question, "Where shall I sleep tonight?" the guard with the slanted eyes replied, "Don't worry, there'll be a bed," and slammed the door. The woman did not talk; the only sign of life was her large brown eyes, which because of her pale face, seemed particularly dark.

Maiga explained that this woman was operated on a few hours earlier. Aha, I thought to myself, she was placed here for me to nurse, as Maiga hardly ever left her bed. I was not worried about where to sleep, because there was enough room for a third bed along the empty wall on the right. Later our new patient became restless, moving her lips, asking for something to drink. Since a mug of cold tea stood beside her, I held the mug to her lips.

The patient drank eagerly, taking small sips. After the drink she was calm for about an hour. Then she experienced shortness of breath. I pounded the door with my fists. Nobody came. I removed my shoe and pounded on the door with the heel. Finally the guard with the slanted eyes opened the feeding window and threatened me, "What, have you gone insane? Do you want the punishment cell?"

Quick, call the doctor, oxygen bag, quickly," I shouted.

"The doctor will be here tomorrow," he said and slammed the window. I pounded the door even more desparately, because the woman was growing worse. The guard yelled, "Stop it, or you will go to the punishment cell at once."

"The woman is dying, call the nurse."

Again he slammed the window with a bang and went to the other end of the hallway. The nurse heard my pounding and came on her own. She returned with the oxygen bag quickly. I put the bag to the woman's lips and she seemed to take a couple breaths. The nurse took the woman's hand to check her pulse. The woman was no longer breathing. We closed her eyes. Immediately two prisoners, stretcher-bearers, appeared. We stood for a couple of minutes in silence, then the dead woman was placed on the stretcher and carried away.

A few days later a nurse explained what happened to the woman who died in my bed. A Russian, she was arrested, operated on, and died, all on the same day. The militia, arriving at her house to arrest her, found her severely beaten by her husband. She left two small children at home. The militia brought her directly to prison, because of her serious condition. She was examined and operated on for an internal hemorrhage. Nothing could be done because her spleen had been detached. Sewn up and put into my bed, she was not expected to live until the evening. Because I am leery about beds in which someone has died, I did not sleep much during the following nights.

Nothing special occured in the next few days. Then came the day when my sentence was pronounced: Four years in the severe regime corrective labor camp for anti-Soviet propaganda. When I returned as a sentenced prisoner I was moved to a different ward in the hospital. Maiga, the "broody hen," could question another with her honeyed, flattering smoker's voice.

I was placed in the maternity ward, a larger room with eight beds: seven pregnant women and me. Six of them were Russians, the seventh, a Gypsy. The Gypsy was sentenced to two years for speculation, the rest were sentenced for theft.

I did not remain with the pregnant women long. In a week I was transferred to the fourth block, as my treatment was supposed to be finished.

CHAPTER 6

THE FOURTH BLOCK

Those who have been sentenced are placed in the fourth block. These wards are exactly the same as in the preliminary investigation block, with one difference: There is ink on the table. The sentenced prisoner is allowed to have a pencil, paper, and other writing materials.

As in the preliminary investigation ward, the majority of the inmates were young Russians. All the Latvians, except two, were former bookkeepers who received relatively stiff sentences, from five to ten years. One received twelve years. One of the other Latvians was a young woman named Livija who had a narrow face, amiable eyes, and a pleasant, quiet voice. Despite being seven months pregnant, she was sentenced by the Soviet court for giving false witness.

Livija tried to defend her friend Erna who was on trial. Although the friend confessed, Livija's denial angered the judge, who ordered Livija's arrest despite her pregnancy. Erna received twelve years. Unable to alter her friend's fate, Livija gained a year in prison where her daughter was born. Livija was sentenced to prison because of her good heart. Ilga, the other Latvian, should not have been in prison either. Ilga, her husband Arnis, and another young man, Janis, attempted to cross the border into Finland on foot. They obtained ski boots, a compass, and food, and traveled by train to Petrozavodsk. From there they walked across the marshes of Karelia to Finland. Although they followed the compass, they kept returning to the same place. Unbeknownst to them, magnetic fields in the area prevented the compass from working properly.

Then misfortune struck. Despite the bitterly cold winter, unfrozen pools covered only by a thin layer of ice remain in the Karelian marshes. Since the whole marsh was covered with snow, these pools were impossible to detect. While walking along the white, snow covered plain, Ilga felt the ground give way under her. There was nothing she could grab. In less than a minute Ilga was up to her shoulders in cold marsh water. Arnis rushed to her with a branch, but he fell through the ice before he could reach her. Both of them were in mortal danger. Fortunately, Janis continued the rescue.

Half an hour elapsed before Janis, thoroughly wet, managed to help Ilga from the pool. Then both of them helped Arnis out. Their clothes were frozen solid. They needed to build a fire to thaw their clothes and save their lives. A fire was risky, because the border guards might see the smoke, but they had no choice.

They removed their outer clothing which they placed by the fire, but the severe frost made it impossible to strip to underwear. Towards evening, Ilga's temperature rose, her face and body burned with pneumonia. With every hour Ilga's condition worsened. Arnis and Janis decided they must find the border guards to save Ilga's life. Janis called, built a fire, but found no trace of any guard. A whole day elapsed before Janis found them, explained Ilga's condition, and asked for help. All three suffered from frostbitten hands and feet.

They were taken to the hospital in Petrozavodsk. Despite every effort, Arnis lost both feet. Janis, only nineteen, lost both hands and feet in his attempt to reach freedom. Ilga was more fortunate. The high temperature caused by pneumonia kept the heat in her limbs for a longer time and only half of each foot had to be amputated. When all three were out of danger, they were transferred to prison and from there, on a prison transport, to the Cheka's basements in Riga.

Those who sat in the Cheka's basements remember the heavy sounds from the hallway at toilet time made by people hobbling on crutches. On my first day in Cheka's cell thirteen, the sounds suggested at least five people on crutches. It was only three, Janis, Ilga, and Arnis. Arnis, the principal offender, was given seven years. Janis, without hands and feet, received five years. Ilga, considered a collaborator, was sentenced to two years.

When she arrived in the ward for sentenced prisoners, Ilga's feet were not yet healed so she was still on crutches. Despite her physical handicap, Ilga's spirit could not be broken. She courageously demanded that the prison administration observe at least the minimal rights of the prisoners. At times great arguments arose between Ilga and the prison guards. Placement in the punishment cell, with which she was repeatedly threatened, endangered her health. Once she was placed there, but the prison doctor protested and after a few hours she was removed. Militant and strong, she quickly earned authority and respect in the ward.

The most miserable people were the former bookkeepers and store employees, for whom prison life was difficult. First, they came from comparatively good circumstances; second, in some cases they regretted their crimes; and third and most important, they all had children and husbands at home. They missed their children, but their greatest concern was that their husbands would not wait for them to serve their sentences. Some of them were already weeping over their husbands.

I had not yet met all the inmates when I was told to collect my belongings, as I would be going on the prison transport. In the Soviet Union transport means traveling in a barred railroad car from one place of imprisonment to another. The guard announced it in one breath, emphasizing the word "transport." Although prison guards appear unfeeling towards other people's fates, "transport" was important even for them.

Only in rare cases since 1956 were people sent out of the Latvian republic on a prison transport. They were sent for particularly dangerous state crimes: Treason against the homeland and anti-Soviet propaganda. All other crimes qualify as social crimes and despite ten to fifteen year sentences, these prisoners remainded in Latvia, where there were plenty of punishment camps. After the guard made her announcement and slammed the door, the ward became ominously silent, and all eyes focused on me. I stood, overwhelmed with a strange feeling of happy excitement.

It might seem paradoxical to feel both happy and concerned, especially since "transport" was nothing good. But I was happy to be going, if even to something worse. I assembled my meager prison belongings. I almost felt like singing, but worried what others would think, so I didn't.

I spread my knitted sweater on the table and piled up my two shirts, three pairs of pants, one dress, comb, and toothbrush. Some wardmates thought I did not have enough. A pretty, tall brunette added a carefully folded woolen kerchief to my pile, saying, "That is for your head in cold weather."

Helene Celmina

I felt ill at ease and said, "That is not necessary."

The whole ward came alive. "Of course it's necessary. None of us will go on the transport. We can receive what we need from home."

Since I had been arrested during the summer, my only warm garment was the knitted sweater. By the investigator's orders I could not receive anything from home. Another woman added a woolen scarf. The third put down a pair of socks. Then came a group of women, even the poorest, each with something in her hand: an onion, a handkerchief, mittens, a package of cigarettes, The majority gave packages of cigarettes or mahorka, as every smoker understands another smoker. After my bundle was tied and I was waiting to be taken to the railway car, a Russian, stocky and roundish in stature, about sixty, looked at my white summer shoes. With small, quick steps, she hurried to her corner and rummaged under her bed. She returned with a pair of white felt boots trimmed with brown leather. "Take these from me," she said in Russian. "You can believe me, an old woman, I know what Siberia means and you can't get by without these."

"But these are very expensive boots and I cannot take them," I protested.

"They're not quite new, but good enough for the camp. Better put one on right away, so I can see whether they fit." I tried on one boot which was about a size too large. "It fits!" The old woman cried with delight.

The others advised me, "Be sure and take them, do not refuse a good heart."

I kissed the donor on both cheeks and placed the boots beside my bundle. The prison guard arrived and ordered me to take my things and go. All the women crowded around, to kiss me good-bye and say a few parting words. The kissing took time, and the prison guard impatiently rapped her keys against the steel gratings. However I took my leave properly and when the last prison gate clanged shut, I knew that something unusual was about to start.

I was dazzled, coming from the shadowed prison rooms, into the sunny day. I did not have far to go because one gate led directly from the prison yards to the railroad. This gate had obviously been built long ago, when masses of people were deported. I crossed several tracks to reach the prison car with barred windows. The car contained what appeared to be animal cages. I was placed into one of these. I asked where I would be taken, and was told I did not need to know. I settled myself more comfortably and waited for what would come next. After a while I felt my car being hooked onto a train. The transport began.

CHAPTER 7

THE STAGE

I often overheard the word "stage" used in conversations: "transported by stage," "the stage has arrived," "just you wait till they move you by stage." I never thought about the meaning of the word, other than transportation of prisoners from one place of imprisonment to another. Now I was going by stage. I thought it was a situation of being moved by train to a new destination either directly, or possibly in stages, involving stopovers to change trains.

I didn't know how long I had been traveling since I never saw a clock. When the train stopped I was told to collect my things and get out. Four soldiers with automatic rifles surrounded me and led me off. We reached Pskov and I was taken to the prison where the thick, almost black walls, always wet, reeked of, if not the Dark Ages, at least century-old dungeons. The Count of Monte Cristo must have been locked in a similar place, I was searched and my things rummaged through, then I was taken to an empty cell, and the door was slammed shut. I was left alone to let my imagination run wild.

Fortunately I was not detained long in this wet fortress. Within a few days I heard a sharp order: "With your things." Happily I jumped up and prepared my bundles. When several hours passed and nobody came, I worried that they had forgotten me. The guards finally came and took me to the train. The car was filthy, and I felt that I would stick to the walls if I touched them. The cars jolted and rolled towards the unknown. This trip took longer than the last.

There were also other prisoners in the car, which was divided into compartments by partitions extending to the ceiling. I was alone in the first compartment, the other prisoners were led aboard from the rear of the car. The doors to the corridor were replaced by prison bars. From their slang I understood that these prisoners derived their livelihood from bur-

The Stage

glary and robbery. Six or seven of them got out with me. All wore black prison garb. Their shaved heads resembled pumpkins; their unshaven faces sprouting like cactuses.

One stopped near me. His face inspired horror. His eyes were frightening, set unnaturally high in his forehead, almost at the hairline which was visible despite the shaven head. One could not tell the color of his eyes since they were set deeply, like a prehistoric man. His cap was pushed far back, fully exposing the horrible face. Two gaping nostrils substituted for the nose while the mouth extended from ear to ear like a lizard or frog. The faces of the others could not be distinguished, being shaded by the bill of the cap. They seemed always to pull down the caps all the way forward, with the front resting on the bridge of the nose. I couldn't figure out how they didn't stumble because the caps appeared well over the eyes.

Everybody stepped forward when his name was called out, and recited his given name, patronymic, and the length of his sentence. Then we moved slowly across the tracks towards the closed-in prison van, accompanied by dogs and guards. In the distance I noticed the station was named Kostroma. Shop windows in Riga displayed huge yellow wheels, labelled "Kostroma Cheese." Thinking of cheese made me suddenly hungry, since for days I existed on dry bread and water. The van, like the train, was subdivided into several barred partitions, and I was placed in the rear partition with the guards. The other criminals were put into the front, as far inside as possible.

Two guards and a dog got into the back, the commander of the convoy with all the papers climbed up with the driver. The van started, however the road was so bad that the van seemed about to tip over any moment. Except for the rattles and the squeaking wheels the motion was like being at sea in a storm. All of a sudden somebody asked in clear Latvian "What city are you from?" I started from my nautical dreams and turned toward the voice, one of the guards at the back.

"From Riga," I replied, then asked, "Do you have to be in the Army much longer?"

With a sigh he replied, "A whole year. But what are you here for?"

"Because of anti-Soviet propaganda, dear friend."

"I feel for you. A month ago several others from Riga were brought here. They were also Latvians . . . all for politics."

"Oh, I know them. Don't you know where they're taking us?"

"I don't really know, but I've heard it might be Abakan-Taishet."

Conversation was difficult because we had to talk softly so the commander would not hear. The rattle of the van created a racket. The other soldier, smoking and spitting, gazed out of the window. We could not talk once we arrived at the prison gates. I was surprised at how nice this yard looked. Trees displayed their luxuriant spring greenery, and flower beds with green shoots and an odd pansy ran along the prison walls. I was received by a smiling woman guard who looked me over and proudly announced that the bath was ready. I was surprised by her tone, which suggested I had come to visit for a few days. I answered, "Naturally, I'm just visiting, no chance of staying on. They'll be taking us further tomorrow or the day after. Who knows when I'll get another chance to take a sauna."

I liked this woman. She showed me my cell where I dropped my things. The cell was built of wood, even the cot was wood, painted dark green. The chamber pot, a barrel, was also wood, in the same dark green oil paint with two metal handles, one on each side, and a wooden lid. The floor had been scrubbed clean white, like the bare board floors scrubbed in the Latvian countryside on Saturday nights. I put down my things, picked up a clean change of clothes and asked, "What about soap?"

"There is enough soap in the sauna. If you want to wash anything you can do that at the same time."

As I opened the door to the sauna the air was pleasantly warm and dry. The guard pointed out everything. "Bang on the door when you're finished," she said, shutting and bolting the door behind me. A large bluish white-washed stove loomed on the right. As I got closer, shiny brown cockroaches took fright and scattered into the cracks, only their long feelers waving outside. The sauna was homey, with wooden benches, dry and clean, in two rows. At one end were several stacks of traditional galvanized sauna wash basins, exactly like those in the Riga saunas.

I was extremely pleased with the sauna. Because it was unlike a prison, I tried to stay as long as possible. I finally returned to my cell and heard movement at the cell door. "There's cabbage left from dinner, cold by now, but perhaps you'd like some?" The guard handed me a bowl. Surprised that anybody cared for my welfare, I thanked her. The cabbage soup tasted foul; still I ate more than half. Silence and peace prevailed in the Kostroma fortress. It seemed as if I was the only one here.

Next morning, after tea, I was taken into the exercise yard, a simple bare patch of ground, with a fence around it. There were no watch towers with guards. No one watched while I walked. In the grassy strip along the fence dandelions bloomed. Summer was coming. After one more day in this "friendly prison" at Kostroma, the order, "with your things," was barked out. I was the last one aboard the van and got more fresh air because there was no door at the back, just bars.

We arrived at the railroad tracks where the convoy with dogs awaited. Once we were put into the cages, the train began to move. The trip to Yaroslavl passed quickly. Again the name of the city matched that of a cheese, a round oblong cylinder, like a log of sawn wood. The prison at Yaroslavl compared to that at Kostroma was a real prison with massive iron gates and thick walls. No greenery nor flowers were visible. Here all the guards were men. My bag was barely opened, then slammed shut, and I was ordered to follow the guards to my cell. The block I was taken to felt chilly and smelled of steel and damp walls.

Except for a small light in the ceiling the cell seemed absolutely bare. Only later did I see the bed; a steel frame with bars, locked to the wall during the daytime. When unlocked, the frame formed a shelf which did not touch the floor. Not knowing that prisoners on the "stage" were not entitled to mattresses or bedclothes, I knocked on the door. When the guard appeared I pointed at the widely spaced grating that was my bed and asked for a mattress. The guard angrily stared at me and then snapped, "Not entitled to any. It's no hotel here." Then, as hard as he could, he slammed the door. I tried moving this way and

that, but there was no position in which I could comfortably
spend more than ten minutes. The sparse straps pressed into
my ribs, and my legs an arms kept dangling through the bars.
Finally I sat down on the concrete floor, with my back against
the wall. The clanging of keys woke me up. A different prison
guard, an elderly man, stood in the doorway. He asked, "Why
aren't you sleeping?" I growled "You show me how to lie down
on this grating."

"Probably it can't be done," he muttered. "You should
have asked for a mattress during the day. Now the
storeroom's closed."

"I asked for it, but they wouldn't give it to me."

"Well, that's true. You're not entitled to it, but one
could make an exception for a woman," the guard added.
However, I spent the whole night sitting on the floor.
Next day the command, "with your things," came as a
relief.

The stage this time was large, holding about fifty of us, more
women than men. Thirty women were pushed into two
crowded compartments. In order to attract the attention of the
men, they started to sing, one with a particularly good voice.
Then they started to look for "relatives," asking in loud voices
for names and birthplaces. The day was already warm and it
became stifling in the car. Finding it hard to breathe, the
women started to yell and bang against the doors, asking for
water. Then somebody remembered me.

"Who's that monkey, sitting all alone in her cage? Let
us in there boss, there's no air in here."

"We're suffocating," somebody else growled.

"What's up, are you deaf that you can't hear us?"
someone squealed.

Then another asked more politely, "Eh, boss, please
let us into the front compartment, we'll be good." Several

women kept on haggling but no one answered. Gradually the whole car quieted down, except for an occasional curse.

When I was brought some drinking water, I asked the soldier where we were going. "To Kirov," he answered. Seeing that nobody was near, he asked, "Tell me, you're in for spying, aren't you?"

"Where did you get that from?" I asked brusquely. "I looked, out of curiosity, at your document envelope. Naturally we're not allowed to open them, but the outside of the envelope says paragraph sixty-five."

Now things made sense. In the legal code of the Soviet Union, paragraph sixty-five deals with spying. But in the code of the Lativan Republic the same paragraph deals with "anti-Soviet agitation." I explained this discrepancy.

"I see. Please excuse my curiosity, but I'm interested in what you agitated about."

"Absolutely nothing," I answered with a smile. But because he was interested and his tone was polite, I explained in detail how I had been reading foreign literature in Swedish, English, and German, which the KGB afterwards labeled anti-Soviet.

This soldier's interest increased. He looked left and right and asked again softly, almost whispering, *"Sprechen Sie Deutsch?"* I asked him in German why he wanted to know so much. In good accented German he replied that he was a German teacher. Our conversation was cut off by someone approaching down the corridor. Later, he tossed a few cigarettes through the bars into my lap. They were better than those I had received as a farewell gift at the Riga jail.

The train stopped. After it started to move again, the teacher stopped by again and handed me three packs of Bulgarian "Shipka" cigarettes which he bought at the station, especially for me. Then, in German he told me the story of his life. He told me his name was Ruslan, he was twenty-five years old and single. He was from the Azerbaijanian city Baku, and although it was abhorrent for him to serve in the Russian army, there was nothing he could do about it.

I felt that there was a lot he would have liked to talk about, but could not for fear of personal jeopardy. The shift changed, and Ruslan returned to his compartment. In the morning he returned to my cage and speaking softly, gave me an address in Baku which I memorized.

After a few hours we reached Kirov. The prison at Kirov had wooden gates, a green yard, and low blue-painted wooden fences encircling flowerbeds. There were barracks on both sides of the road: They were simple wood frame barracks, painted light blue with red and green embellishments, surrounded by lilacs in bloom. I was amazed at the bright colors. The prison looked like a market place full of booths. This farcical impression was emphasized by the satirical wall board labeled "Crocodile" nailed to one wall.

I was led to a large house behind the barracks, up wooden stairs to the second floor, to a tiny cell. Although empty at the moment, it was designed for two, judging by the two-tier bed. Not ten minutes passed before somebody knocked on the wall. Because one never knows who's on the other side of the wall, I returned the call. I heard a voice coming from the window. The window had normal bars in front of it, without boards or screens. The voice told me to go to the bars. I climbed up to the top bunk to reach them. Then the voice asked me to stick my hand through the bars. Into my hand fell a thick piece of string, pulled taut by a ball of dried bread at the end. "And now, pull it," the voice ordered. I pulled, and to my amazement found a pack of cigarettes attached to it. I thanked him. The string disappeared as suddenly as it appeared. I asked how he knew that I smoked. "All pretty girls smoke," he answered.

I asked how he knew what I looked like, and he told me that he looked at me with his mirror. At first I could not figure out how he could have a mirror in prison, but then I realized that on our arrival, nobody even looked at our bags. Jangling keys and thumping steps interrupted my thoughts. The noise stopped outside my door. Two women who arrived on another "stage" train were brought in. I pointed out that there were only two beds in our cell. "You're going to make it, somehow," we were told. As we began to get acquainted, the door opened again. A woman guard, stepping almost inside our cell asked, softly so that no one from adjacent cells could hear, "Girls, do any of you have clothes to sell? Tomorrow morning I will bring sugar, white bread, bacon . . . whatever you want in the way of goods."

I was confused and amazed by such unheard of behavior by a prison guard. She continued "Don't be afraid, I'll pay for everything we agree to, right here on the spot. You see, here we don't have knitted cardigans, nor woolen head scarves. We can get nothing here." The scarves I received as presents were not what she wanted, but one of the other women did have an imported cardigan that was to the guard's liking. Since they could not agree on a price, the guard wanting it practically for nothing, no transaction took place. The guard left with her feelings hurt.

We continued to get acquainted. The elder woman, who had been negotiating over her cardigan, was well into her sixties, plump, active, and moved with the agility and grace of a much younger woman. She was well dressed, her clothes obviously obtained on the black market. When asked why she was in prison, she answered, "For practicing palmistry and chiromancy."

"And for how long?"

"I got seven years, since it's my second time under the same paragraph."

"I've never heard of anybody getting sentenced for predicting the future by reading somebody's palm."

"And how! I'm telling you, it's my second time already. I became too famous. My services were in high demand by too many fine ladies."

The other, younger new-arrival remarked, "But surely you could have read your own fortune well in advance, and then gone to a far away place where no one would know you. Russia's so big."

"You cannot escape fate anywhere, daughter," the fortuneteller replied sagely.

The younger woman, an Ossetin, was alarmingly beautiful or, more precisely, wildly and exotically beautiful. Her skin tone was quite dark, and her long hair was jet black, arranged in a thick braid lying like a snake on her back. Her eyebrows, too, were jet black, curved as if drawn by an especially skillful make-up artist. Her most alarming features were her eyes, black, and in the shade of long eyelashes, unnaturally large and almost threatening. I became uneasy, almost fearful looking into her eyes for any length of time. Despite being frightened by her eyes, like a doomed rabbit standing fixed before a snake, I could not help looking at her.

Dinner time arrived. The little window in the door opened, and two friendly young men, obviously inmates, offered us fish. I thought they were pulling a morbid practical joke on us new arrivals, gullible enough to believe anything. I was amazed when I went to the window and received a beautiful piece of boiled cod in a aluminum bowl.

"A pity there's no bread to go with it," I must have thought aloud.

"How's that? No bread? I'll get you some in a minute." The young man ran away and returned a moment later with bread. I thanked them repeatedly. I kept eating and praising the food, "Where did they find excellent fish like this in Kirov, so far from the sea, when they only gave us heads and fishbones in the prison in Riga?"

My cellmates agreed that it was unusual to receive such good fish in prison. We ate, licking our fingers and sucking the bones. I divided the bread so that we each got equal shares. Then the window opened again and the men asked if we wanted extra helpings. We yelled yes in unison, and I asked what was the occasion to be getting such good food.

"No occasion at all, its just something for you, pretty girls, from us, the men from Kirov." He handed us a bowl of fish. Naturally, we smiled and were happy.

"God bless you and give you health," the old woman wished him. The window closed, and we feasted and praised these decent boys.

"A strange prison," I mused, "they have great freedom here. Nowhere else are prisoners allowed to distribute food to other inmates."

"And in the prison at Gorki I never saw another prisoner for four years," added the brunette.

"How's that, didn't see anybody? You're not saying you spent four years in solitary?" I asked, amazed.

"Yes in solitary."

"The investigation took that long?"

"No, that was part of my sentence. They brought a sewing machine into my cell, where I sat and sewed because my sentence called for the first four years to be spent in a prison. Those four years have passed, and I'm being taken by stage to a forced labor camp."

Spending time in solitary with a sewing machine was unheard of.

"Do you have much time left now?"

"Long enough to leave this place as an old bag. I was given fifteen, now I'm twenty-nine. When I was imprisoned I was twenty-five."

"What for?"

"For murder," she stated simply.

"Who did you kill?"

"Who else but a man. My sentence wouldn't have been nearly as severe if the bastard had been a civilian, but unfortunately he was an officer."

"Yes, you're right, only seven or eight years for a civilian," I added compassionately.

"In no way more than ten," the black-eyed beauty agreed.

She asked what chiromancy was. The old woman explained that she predicted the future from the stars, from lines in the palm of one's hand, and that she was also well versed in many other fields. Naturally, the black-eyed beauty asked the old woman to predict her future. The palm reader excused herself because of weak eyesight and the poor light in the cell.

At bedtime, the palm reader because of her size needed a bed to herself. We, the two skinny ones, shared the other bed. I felt somewhat uncomfortable sharing a bed with a strange woman, a murderer at that. She fell asleep quickly, while I lay awake.

When I finally slept, I had crazy nightmares: I dreamed I was under the spell of a sorceress, an old woman with a big black eyes that blazed youthfully. When she looked at me she lowered her brows and lashes like window blinds. She ordered me to look in her eyes. The longer I looked the more I saw, like looking at a television set. I saw vison after vision that I could not have thought on my own. She told me to swing my arms around and around, and to fly off into the moonlit night. I obeyed and took off steeply like a helicopter. However high I rose, her eyes remained before me. They glowed with a fascinating, luminescent sheen under the large fans formed by her lashes. Then a strange cosmic music started; it sounded like avant-garde jazz and changed into clanking.

When I opened my eyes I understood the clanking. The prison guard walked down the corridor, banging the keys against the steel door fittings, loudly shouting, "Get up, get up." My bedmate on the outside jumped out of the bed. Her black braid had come apart and the wavy hair covered her back. Though to Russian taste she was not quite plump enough, nevertheless, the guards still found this black-eyed girl appealing. Every now and then the door opened and a couple of men stood in the entrance staring at her. Word about the rare specimen in cell number four spread quickly through the jail because after breakfast, the highest prison administrators came to inspect her. The door opened to admit four officers in Ministry of the Interior uniforms. There was not room for four, so one stepped across the threshold and entered our cell. Making a show of being on a fact-finding mission they questioned her about her sentence, prison work, etc. Then they shook their heads over the fact that she still had to spend so many years in confinement. "Poor girl," one of them said leaving. This "poor girl" had killed someone, yet everyone felt sorry for her.

The window was opened by yet another man. "Do you want to take a walk?" he asked, "if you do then get ready." An old guard took us to the exercise yard. He ordered two more cells opened, releasing seven more prisoners. Against prison rules, he took us out together. The old guard did not stare at the black-eyed girl, but took us by a long fence, grayed by natural weathering, in contrast to the gaily painted fences at the front of the prison. We came to a small padlocked gate in the middle of the fence. While the guards unlocked the padlock I heard voices behind the fence. We entered a small yard containing about ten women, some walking around, some squatting on the ground, all talking animatedly.

The prison inmates rapidly quizzed each other, "Where are you from?" and "Where are you going?" This collection of information was to find out about their friends. They wanted to know who gained freedom, and who returned to prison after how long a period, who traveled on which "stage," which breaches of rules were committed, and how many times someone was in solitary confinement. Most important was to discover who was eating with whom, at this revealed relationships, including intimate ones. The three of us were not from the right category. In addition, we came from prisons and not forced labor camps, which meant no information could be gained from us. I got to know only one woman among this motley crowd. She was in for murder and had been sentenced a long time ago. She traveled by "stage" from her camp far away in the Urals to her native city of Dnepropetrovsk as a witness in another court case. She told me that she came from a special camp in the Perm district in the Urals. This camp at Bereznyki was solely for women sentenced for murder. I asked if this camp held many inmates.

"A little more than a thousand," she explained.

"It would be interesting to know if anybody was from Latvia."

"Yes, we have two, one a very intelligent lady from Riga." she announced with pride then gave her name.

"I know, I know!" I exclaimed. "I've heard about that case. It was rather mysterious, and apparently the guilt was never quite proved."

"She says she's not guilty." My partner emphasized the word, "not." "But the murdered man's mother pointed the finger at her in court, asking for the death penalty," she added.

"Yes, people at the hearing said the same thing, but nobody clearly understood what actually happened. Those who know her agree that she couldn't be guilty and must have been promised a large sum of money to accept the blame."

At length, and in some detail, she started to tell me about herself: "I met an officer who appeared to be a decent and quiet guy from another city. He settled in the end room of my uncle's house, which was small. I was then of the age to be 'given away.' Having looked me over, he came to our place with wine to propose to me. All my relatives were delighted with my marriage to an officer. We celebrated our wedding and went on living reasonably. After a year I had a son, later a daughter."

"Old folks say one shouldn't marry a stranger, one never knows what devils may possess him. My neighbors opened my eyes more and more frequently, saying that he was seen here and there. Often he wouldn't come home nights. When I asked him where he was, he always answered, 'A military secret.' What could I do?"

"One morning he was hungover and would not wake up. Then my son, already two, went to the chair over which my husband's uniform was hanging. He stuck his hand into the pocket of the uniform and pulled out two letters, one was crumpled up. I shouted to my son not to touch his daddy's papers. As if the devil himself pulled me over to have a look, I picked up the envelope. I took out the letter and the photo of a rather pretty woman with two little boys on her lap. I started to read but did not understand. The more I read, the less I understood. I turned the letter over without having read it to the end, and saw, 'Kisses, your wife, Nyura.' Tears clouded my eyes. I had to know more. I wiped my eyes and started again from the beginning. 'Haven't your maneuvers finished by now? How long should I wait for you? Four years have passed. And you send me so little money, how are we supposed to make ends meet? Thank you at least for not forgetting me on my birthday by sending me the beautiful ruby brooch.'"

The woman continued, "A hot current passed down my back. I jumped up, as if stung, to look in the desk drawer. My only memento from my dead mother, a brooch with two tiny rubies, was missing. I looked at my husband, sleeping off his hangover. He reeked so strongly of rotten fish and vodka that I held my breath ten feet away. At this moment he seemed so repulsive to me, as if I had never seen him before. An overpowering hatred came over me because he deceived me about his other marriage; because of all the nights of 'military secrets;' and finally because of my mother's brooch. I looked through the window where my boy played in the sand pile at the other end of the yard. The little one slept in the cradle."

"I rushed out to the porch where we split wood, grabbed the ax and, not thinking of anything except how much I hated this bastard, I ran to the bed and swung the ax into the sleeper's neck. He never even moved. I was in such a state I couldn't look at the bed. I yanked the baby from her cradle, grabbed the boy in the yard, and ran as if pursued straight to the militia. I was dead tired and I did not understand what was happening. I sat down and started to scream for 'help.' They called the local medic who injected something, and I told them everything."

She started to cry. Even now, what happened still moved her although over a year passed.

"Who is taking care of the children?" I asked her, lighting a cigarette. My hands shook because her story touched me so deeply

"The children have it good, thanks to God. They are at my sister's. She loves children. One time, when I was in my native town, the children were brought over to see me. They had grown." She wiped her tears. "I went back once again to testify about my husband's sins. He and friends falsified papers at a warehouse to get money for drinking."

"How much were you given?"

"I got by with seven years. After all, in your native town you are known from your school days on. They knew I wouldn't have committed such a crime if that stranger hadn't turned up. The Army staff also gave him a bad character reference wherever he went."

The exercise period was intended for walking and muscle stretching. Engrossed in this tragic story, we sat down on the ground with our backs against the fence. And now, when we both decided to move and stretch our legs, the guard opened the gate and announced that our walk period was over. We moved toward the exit as we had been taught ever since our first days in prison, in single file, with our hands on our backs.

After lunch the black-eyed girl successfully twisted the palm-reader's arm. I regarded this fortunetelling as futile and doubted her ability. In order not to hurt her feelings I stuck my hand out saying, "While you are at it, please see what's ahead for me." She looked and told me that I could expect to be arrested again around 1970. Not wanting to believe this, I lost all interest.

The window opened and a guard we had not seen before yelled out, "Is there anyone here who'd want to come over to the guards' hut to wash the floor?" I volunteered. One cannot pass up such an opportunity to find valuable things, like a pencil stub, a match or a piece of razor blade which are useful in barter. The guard evaluated me from head to toe and asked, for security reasons, how many years I received. "I was given four. One I've sat off, three remain now."

"Good," he said, "let's go."

I grabbed the knitted sweater and followed him through the well-cared-for prison garden where the male inmates worked as gardeners. They wanted to get acquainted, not knowing I was not "one of them." Only after I crossed the entire courtyard without answering did someone say, "She's not one of ours."

Washing the floor was successful. I carried water from the other end of the hut where there was a kitchen where visitors to the inmates could prepare meals. A woman was forming pelmens, the large, Siberian dumplings filled with meat. She automatically asked me, "For how many years, where from and what for?" I answered in similar shorthand that I was in for politics. I could not stand and talk for any length of time, although nobody was checking on me. Therefore I went to change the water as often as possible. The woman was visiting her son who received two years under the paragraph for hooliganism, applied to fighting. The woman regretted that she could not offer me anything, because the pelmens would not be ready in less than an hour.

I did find some useful things while washing the floor: a small mirror, two hair clips, and a match box with a piece of lipstick. When I went to change the water the third time, the woman rushed forward with something white. "Here take it, it's sugar. My son has enough, I brought him plenty of everything. I live close by, you're from far away." All this she poured out in a single breath. She did not have any paper, so the sugar lay in big lumps in her calloused hands as in a bowl. "Quick," she said, "take it, before somebody comes."

I put the lumps of sugar in my blouse. Only the thin layer of my slip kept the sugar away from my body. The sugar lumps fell on top of each other, forming a big bulge around my midriff. In the meantime the bucket had filled with water. Thanking her for her generosity, I returned to my work. I yanked on my cardigan to conceal the bulges. Whenever I moved the lumps rustled but could not be seen. Back in my cell I wrapped my sugar in a large clean handkerchief. First I offered a piece to each of my cell-mates, who already had sugar.

We spent one more night sleeping as a threesome. Then early in the morning they called for me "with your things." The others remained behind another few days. In the "stage" block of the Kirov prison, as in a hotel, the inmates stayed only a few days, until the next "stage" car.

I crossed the verdant yard as slowly as possible in order to remember the lilacs in bloom, the decorative shrubs, and the flowers. Awaiting me was a locked prison van, tracks, a barred car, surrounded by soldiers with automatics slung around their necks and a couple of dogs on short leashes.

The cages in the barred car were not as overcrowded as the last time. Nevertheless a middle-aged woman with two sacks of things was put into my cage when the train stopped. She was angry and would not talk. She appeared not to have been in for more than a week. She seemed resentful towards her situation and was put off the train in the middle of the night.

I traveled alone and learned from a soldier that we were going to Sverdlovsk. The trip was long and tiring. Finally we arrived at a gloomy and depressing prison where discipline and order ruled. Our things were examined carefully, and we were meticulously checked for lice. Then we were taken to the bathroom.

I was let into the bathroom with a Chinese woman. I disrobed and began to wash. The Chinese woman kept on a long white broadcloth shirt and her leather boots. I thought she feared that someone might steal her boots, for she entered the sauna wearing both shirt and boots. The sauna was bleak: a large concrete room with exposed iron pipes above, fitted every three feet with the head of a watering can. We could not adjust the water ourselves; this was done by the sauna assistants, male inmates. They asked us through the glassless window how we wanted the water, and then adjusted the taps accordingly. The Chinese woman may have known about the spectators in the Sverdlovsk jail and perhaps that is why kept her shirt and boots on. I kept my back towards the window, washed my hair, and left as soon as possible. Then I was given a medical examination.

On the way to my cell, the guard explained that the large prison was built in the days of Catherine the Great. Seen from above, it forms her initial "E." (Catherine, written in Russian starts with an "E.") The prison was intended as a maximum security jail for those guilty of serious crimes. When the door to my cell opened, I was surprised to find the Chinese woman.

The cell was small and gloomy, with two beds, one along each wall. The rest of the room was bare, without chair or table. The walls were covered in dark grey oil paint to prevent prisoners from writing on the walls, leaving messages for friends. I could not help thinking that the Sverdlovsk authorities were breaking one rule by putting me into a cell with someone else. According to the standing instructions, I, as a particularly dangerous criminal aginst the state, should be kept alone. I was not surprised at Kirov since they did not go by the book on any point.

However, when the Chinese put a finger on her chest, saying "Chu Uh Shi," it was clear that she could not speak Russian and that the Sverdlovsk administration had nothing to fear. I could not indoctrinate her with anti-Soviet ideas, nor could she spoil me with Mao's teachings. For the first time in my life I could not make myself understood. Since I speak several languages I have always been able to communicate through one of them. Chu Uh Shi started to eat her dinner, a large herring and some black bread. She offered a piece of herring to me, too, having deftly skinned it with a spoon. I accepted, thinking one piece would not hurt me. The herring tasted great, later however, I paid for it. Around midnight an excruciating pain hit me and I started to groan. Chu Uh Shi banged on the door. A nice medical aide in a white smock brought me opium and also gave me a shot. The drugs helped and I fell asleep. The aide even prescribed a diet for me.

I knew that eventually I was to be taken to Abakan-Taishet. Then I was told that I had been taken in the wrong direction, because there was no longer a camp at Taishet for the people sentenced according to the code paragraphs as mine. That camp had been moved long ago. I wondered how the administration of the Riga prison did not know where to send me. Several people were already sent from Riga to Taishet, and they turned up in Sverdlovsk again. This time I was to be sent in the "right" direction.

The same night Chu Uh Shi and I were both called "with your things." As we were taken into the corridor a group of minors were brought in from the "stage" through another door.

There were about twenty boys between the ages of fourteen and eighteen. They were dressed in dirty clothes and were bouncy and full of life. Most of them were from orphanages. They were horsing around, not suspecting that few of them would lead normal lives. It was a depressing sight, seeing young children on the way towards a hopeless future. In prison they were taught a trade, and kept working. They provide the state with a cheap source of labor, working their entire lives for the minimum calories required to maintain existence.

The head of the convoy placed me in the car all alone. Chu Uh Shi was placed with the other criminals "against social norms." There I also saw four old Chinese men. Overall, the "stage" from Sverdlovsk was large, all compartments stuffed to capacity. There was no indication of where the train was going.

I fell asleep with my feet towards the inside of the compartment, and my head near the bars. In the middle of the night, I felt someone pulling my hair. In the darkness I could barely see the soldier who yanked my hair. He stood glued against the door to my compartment. He said, "Hurry up." Only when I sat up did I understand. The soldier opened his trousers, pressed his stomach against the bars and stuck his penis through.

"Get lost," I said.

"Look here, stupid, at these goodies," he said.

"I'm going to give your goodies such a kick that you're going to forget what your name is." Finally he backed off, muttered something under his breath and left. The remainder of the night I could not sleep but squatted in the corner, with my chin on my knees and my coat over my legs.

A few of us, including all the Chinese, were put off in Kazan. The prison at Kazan had previously been a Greek Orthodox church. I was taken into a large empty hall filled with double tiered bunks. I waited in vain for Chu Uh Shi to appear. Despite it being summer the room was cool; I was freezing. I put on everything that could provide warmth, yet I was still cold. As prescribed for travelers on the "stage," I slept on the bare bars of my cot with a bundle of clothes as a pillow. Despite not having slept much the previous night, I could not sleep because of the cold. Towards morning I fell asleep briefly but was awakened by the cooing of pigeons. To loosen my limbs, stiff from the cold, I walked up and down the cell. At the same time I counted the beds, sixty, the same number as in Riga. I tried to read the by-laws and rules written on the wall in Russian and in Tatar. On the adjacent wall, however, I found some words penciled in Latvian, "Greetings compatriot" followed by initials.

With the start of the working day the Tatars came to see me. The Tatar prison guards were extremely curious. Some came into my cell, sat down on the edge of an empty bed, and asked about the availability of potatoes, fruit, and meat in Riga, and the prices. Once their curosity was satisfied, I was taken out for a walk. The exercise yards were arranged like triangular slices of pie, cut radially, with the guard positioned at the center, with a little roof above his head. Standing at the narrow end of a yard one could see a corner of the church, the present prison.The walls were plastered white, the slate roof painted dark green. Except for the high fence with the towers and barbed wire, nobody would have thought this building anything but a church. I warmed up outside and was sorry to return to the dark cell. Officially everybody is entitled to one hour of walking. But there is no way inmates can verify their actual time, since they no longer have watches and there are no clocks anywhere in the corridors, let alone in the cells.

From the Tatar capital of Kazan I was taken on a short trip to Ruzayevka where a huge "stage" awaited. It took time before they finished calling our names. Throughout my long travels by "stage," I heard only a handful of non-Russian names, of the black-marketeers from China and Central Asia. The rest had typically Russian surnames. As the names were called, one man attracted everybody's attention and admiration. He was tall, with a masculine face, about forty. When his turn came to give his father's name, the code paragraph and the length of his sentence, everybody listened spellbound to his recital. His paragraphs followed each other closely, as if he was reading from a book, his voice magnificent and loud. He paused for effect, then solemnly announced, "The total term: one-hundred-and-forty years."

Everybody admired him. I wondered how he could get one-hundred-and-forty years. Assuming that the court gave the maximum twenty-five years, he would have to have committed twelve murders in jail, since ten years were added for each one. For camp inmates the years added for crimes committed in camp could not increase the total sentence to more than twenty-five years. It would have been interesting to hear his life story.

In Ruzayevka the station was close, just across the tracks. A whole crowd of us went there. Sapped of my strength, I could no longer carry my leather trunk. The head of the convoy ordered one inmate to walk alongside and carry my trunk. By the time everyone was stuffed as tightly as possible into the cages aboard the van, there was no room for me. The entire stage was made up of men and I was the only woman. I was placed in the middle of the van, between the cages. The trip was over rough road, and the wheels seemed hexagonal, not round. We had not traveled far before I noticed that I had been robbed. I did not notice when my handkerchidf was removed from my coat pocket. Later the man waved it inside the cage. Since it was my only one, I asked for it back. The thieves grinned and laughed. What was I to do? This was their profession.

At Ruzayevka I was taken into a large cell with huge double-tiered bunks along the walls. The cell was overcrowded with women of different ages. Some were lively like wound up springs, while others lolled listlessly on their cots. Another sat on the floor with her back propped against the wall and with the aid of a hair pin, smoked the last fraction of an inch of her cigarette. The moment I stepped over the threshold and bid them good morning, four or five of them surrounded me to ask if I had anything to sell. I told them nothing but sugar.

"What d'you want for the sugar?"

"Cigarettes," I answered.

"All of us want them. You're not going to make a deal."

Then one of them pressed herself close to me and whispered, "It's a pity you don't have earrings. They rate five packs of cigarettes."

"Sorry, but I don't."

"Maybe you've got some lipstick?"

"I've got a little piece," I told her.

"Give it to me."

Suddenly a whole mob milled around, all needing lipstick. I sold it for ten cigarettes and felt pleased. I considered what trinkets I could sell. Here they needed everything. For romance, they wanted to pretty themselves up. They may gain freedom for a short time only, a month at the most. Then they return to their "native home," as prison is called among thieves.

Then the door opened and I was ordered, "with your things." Prison officials committed a grave mistake by failing to look at my paragraph and allowing me to join the other girls. Now I was taken to solitary confinement, as befit my sentence according to the rules.

I was taken to the exercise yard alone, too. On the other side of the fence separating the exercise yards a man was walking. His steps slowed, then stopped. I tried to pretend I was not aware that he was watching me. Then all at once, I heard a kick against the boards, saw two hands appear on top of the fence and watched as the man jumped into my yard. He was young, probably eighteen or nineteen. But to my horror, he seemed to be mad. I was frightened and did not know what to say. Nor did he. He watched me and grinned in a silly way. He came closer, with that grin on his face. To flee seemed futile since the entire yard measured only twenty by ten steps. The gate was locked from outside. I asked his name, and he replied that his name was Misha.

I deliberately spoke loud so the guards would hear. "You sure are a great looking guy, Misha. What on earth are you doing here?"

"Don't you see, they put me into a jail. And they keep beating me." A while later he rubbed his nose into his sleeve and still grinning, continued, "Do you like me?"

"Sure I like you, Misha. Take it easy and relax. I'll talk to the chief and see if I can get him to agree to let you go home."

Overjoyed, he jumped and clapped his hands like a child. "Yes, talk to him," he said, moving closer.

In the meanwhile, the guards noticed that Misha was no longer in his yard. The key clicked and two soldiers grabbed Misha under his arms, ignoring his protests. It is incomprehensible how a sick man can be sentenced to jail. According to the law mental cases are not judged by a court. An individual's ignorance of the law is never allowed as an excuse. But if the state errs and breaks a law, there will always be justification and excuse. I was depressed for several days thinking about the unfortunate Misha.

Ruzayevka serves as a center for the "stages" while its prison functions solely as a transfer jail. Hence it did not insist on strict discipline and one could exchange a word or two with people being taken in the opposite direction. As I was being taken back to my cell, a young man heading for his walk asked me which camp I was going to. I did not know.

"What were you sentenced for?"

"For politics."

"In that case please give my regards to Anna Popowich from Nikolay."

"Where will I see her?"

"She is there, where you are going. You'll recognize her because her right arm is missing."

From Ruzayevka I was taken to Potyma, then the only place where "criminals against the state" or old style "politicals" were kept. A group of particularly dangerous criminals in horizontally striped uniforms were on the same train. We walked across to another track where a narrow-gauge railroad had been constructed to link Potyma with the other camps. Our train had a total of six cars. Everyone boarded and the trip continued. From the car window we saw a camp wherever the train stopped. It looked frightening: a whole region of nothing but camps. Some were very close together, others several miles apart. On the platform of one station I saw Chu Uh Shi and the Chinese group.

Finally I was put off the train. The enclosed prison van took me over rough ground, not a road but a footpath which ran the length of the forest. Frequent use had finally turned it into a rough track. Finally the trip was over, and I was let out at the gate.

CHAPTER 8

CAMP #17 A

In the guard shack a fat woman guard carefully went through my things. When she finished, the door opened and I was admitted into the "zone," a small strip of land, wrenched from the forest, with a road down the middle and white barracks on both sides. The camp was isolated on all sides by a high board fence with several strings of barbed wire attached to the slats. Electrical wires ran along the top of the fence. To the left of the camp was the forest and to the right was the village.

Outside the fence, ground-hugging walls of barbed wire formed an approximately twelve-foot wide strip, while a ten-foot "forbidden zone," separated from the camp proper by a low barbed wire fence, skirted the inside of the fence. The forbidden zone was cleaned, weeded, and smoothed by rake. Every morning and night the camp guard in charge of security walked along the small barbed wire fence to check for footprints within the forbidden zone.

The big camps had observation towers in each corner. However camp #17-A was small (about the size of two soccer fields) and had only two towers. These were placed diagonally opposite each other at the corners so that a guard, standing in a tower, overlooked the fence along two sides. These guards were army draftees who reported to the Ministry of the Interior. Within the compound the guards were either soldiers on extended duty or salaried mercenaries. The women guards were recruited from surrounding villages. All were well paid. The pay in the communal farms was low and the work hard, making the job of a guard much more attractive. The guards in these camps all had a sixth-grade education.

Camp #17-A had a total of four barracks. This included two dormitories and one mess hall, at the end of which was a clinic, a shop, and a storeroom for private belongings. The inmates did not keep their personal items with them in the dormitory, but rather in the storeroom. This arrangement allowed us to rummage through and air our things out on summer Sundays. This pastime reminded us that we, too, once had a different life. In other camps, personal belongings were normally stored outside the zone, the inmates only received them early on the morning of the day they were released. By that time mice may have finished off a shoe, or moths may have eaten holes in coats and woolen scarves.

The fourth barrack was for the administration, containing rooms for those in charge and a sauna. The inmate working in the sauna was disabled, since the able-bodied inmates worked at sewing. The sauna had two rooms: a changing room and a steam room. The sauna contained a huge vat that was filled by means of buckets. The fire under it had to burn for an entire day in order to heat the water. The sauna was heated once every ten days. If inmates wanted, or needed, to wash more frequently, one might dip a half gallon of hot water in a wash

Camp 17-A Steamroom

basin from the large pot built into the floor behind the kitchen. We were allowed to take this water to the barracks at night.

Each of these 120-person barracks contained a small, so-called hygiene room, about five-by-six feet. Often we lined up with our wash basins of warm water, which frequently became cold before we reached the room. The walls, benches, and the small shelf to hold the basins were made of timber. The room was always dark, with long stalked mushrooms growing under the benches in the summertime. During the winter it was cold, since there was no way to heat it. Nevertheless, all of us who had to wash more often than three times a month were glad to have this little hygiene room.

The living quarters were partitioned into two sections, accessible from each end, with a third door mid-way. Each section contained sixty beds. Every two beds were tied together with wire for stability, and being in two tiers, actually formed a block of four beds. Whenever somebody moved in one bed, all four would move and wake up. These four-bed blocks were separated from each other by a three foot strip of floor that contained two small dressers. Each dresser was intended for the personal goods of two people: a mug, a spoon, a comb, a toothbrush, and a couple of books. Spare clothing was kept in the bed under the pillow. The brown bed frames were made of unfinished boards, joined together with large nails.

Every new arrival to the zone received a black cloth bag filled with wood shavings to be used as a mattress, a smaller black bag also filled with wood shaving to be used as a pillow, a dark blue cotton blanket, two sheets, and a pillowcase. Since the women have to wash the sheets themselves, they are issued more soap than the men.The monthly allotment is one piece, or one-half pound per inmate. This piece must be used for washing one's face, hair, clothes, and even occasionally the floor. The entire section contained only one small ceiling light. Whoever wanted to read had to put her head at the foot of her bed, but those in the lower bunks hardly had any light. A small board attached to the foot of each bed gave family name, first name, father's name, and the paragraph and length of the sentence.

A long table covered with a white sheet and with benches on both sides, ran down the middle of the section. On it were newspapers. Food was never allowed at this table which was to be used for political indoctrination read to us by the head of

Helene Celmina

Camp 17-A Hygiene Room

the section. Also inmates were allowed to sit and read at the table during free time. On one side stood a large brick stove, plastered with clay that continually dried and dropped to the floor. Every now and then a piece of dried clay dropped during the night and woke everyone. The stove was heated with coal, a job reserved for the disabled inmates. In the barracks the wood floor had cracks so wide that one had to be careful not to drop anything. Small treasured items like a pencil or a spool of thread that fell down these cracks were lost forever.

During the winter clothes left behind by freed inmates were spread over the cracks. These clothes were taken apart along the seams, stitched together again and spread out evenly to cover the largest possible section of floor. Whenever the wind blew especially hard, it whistled through the cracks and lifted up our rags, as if some phantom had crawled underneath.

The barracks were whitewashed inside and out each spring. Water poured onto the quicklime fizzled like a carbonated drink. We then dipped primitively made grass brushes into the solution. The main thing was to protect one's eyes, as lime burns heal slowly and poorly.

The inmates who had been at the camp from the beginning said that nothing existed in camp #17-A when they arrived. They lived in tents and waited while the men erected the barracks. A barbed wire fence surrounded the tents and conditions were much worse.

Now the work zone was separated from the living zone by a high board fence with a gate in the middle. The work zone contained a long barrack with forty electric sewing machines and also the camp lock-up, a small house surrounded by a triple wire fence. The camp contained two toilets, one in the living and one in the working zones. To the right, beyond the fence was the village where the guards lived with their families, as well as the camp commander and other administrators. The telephone operator lived there, as did the electrician, the medical personnel, the store supervisors, and others. Children, chickens, and pigs all roamed the village without supervision. The white chickens were painted for recognition, some purple while others had green wings or tails. In the middle of the village stood the only water pump, surrounded by a big pool of mud in which pigs and naked children wallowed from dawn to dusk.

Helene Celmina

Whitewashing

CHAPTER 9

THE LATVIANS

It was the work hour, and a young woman wearing glasses came towards me. In clear Latvian she said, "Good day. Erna already told us that you were going to be here soon. My name's Nina, let's get acquainted."

"Where did you get such a Russian name?" I asked.

"Nobody could pronounce my real name so I became Nina ever since childhood. My grandparents owned the dairy in Riga. Because of that all of us were sent to Siberia."

"And how did you get here?"

"That's a long story, however not much is required to get here. Let's go see the Commandant so that she can show you where you're going to be. Give me your case, I'll help you."

She turned out to be strong despite being so tiny. She grabbed my heavy case, and with small running steps, carried it into the barracks. Nina knocked on the Commandant's door, announced me, and, having let me inside, remained outside. The Commandant was about thirty-five, dumpy, wore glasses, and dressed in uniform. Last week's entire menu could be seen on her blouse. She asked for my name and surname and whether I knew how to sew.

She then took me into the section next door where about twenty old women were sitting or lying in their beds. The Commandant asked which beds were not taken. A little old woman stepped forward and pointed out one right in the middle of the room and a couple further away in the dark corners. The Commandant told me to sleep in the middle of the room. A couple of hours later they brought me sheets and blankets from the store and a bag full of wood shavings. I signed for this as if for valuable goods. Two rubles plus a few kopeks per month were to be taken from my salary for the use of my bedclothes. They subtracted a similar amount for room, electricity, food, and uniform. I told them that I had no need for their uniform. "You're wrong, you certainly will need it. Nobody is going to let you walk around in your own clothes," the head of the storeroom, an old man with a wooden leg, solemnly announced.

Then they told me to see the doctor, a short thin captain with dark hair. He hardly spoke beyond asking what was wrong. I told him my physical problems which he wrote down and then solemnly announced: "You will be classified as a Group III disabled person."

Tears rushed to my eyes, I was hardly thirty and they were calling me disabled. I went out and the nurse asked what had happened. "He put me into the disabled category," I mumbled.

"But that's great, you should be overjoyed! That means that you won't have to work at the back-breaking tasks. The doctor knows what he's doing." Only after a month did I understand. Those classified as fully able-bodied sat at the sewing machine for eight hours producing their quota of thirty-two shirts in eight hours.

At night, once work was finished, the first one to rush out and greet me was Erna. While we were talking women returned from the work zone. Most of them walked slowly, weariness visible in every step. A depressing sight, all wore black prison garb, altered to fit, or a mere black shapeless bag with sleeves.

Erna exclaimed, "Zenta, come and meet someone I've told you about. The two of us were locked up together at the Cheka."

We were introduced and I could not help looking at Zenta with horror. She was slightly younger than I. Her face looked waxen, as if yellow parchment were stretched over her skull. Except for her brilliant eyes, it could have been a cadaver's face. Her features were tiny and pretty but the brilliant eyes were unnaturally large. She was tiny and extremely thin. Erna excused herself and ran off. I remained with Zenta.

"I suppose you've been here a long time," I asked with a compassionate voice.

"Yes, I've put quite a few years behind me already," she said with a smile, as if this was nothing worth speaking of. I learned later that she was one of those sentenced to twenty-five years.

When Zenta smiled I noticed that her teeth were made of some dark grey metal. I could not stop myself from asking, "What happened to your teeth? Did they make them like that here?"

"Yes, because they knocked them all out while cross-examining me at the Cheka."

"How did they do that, all at once?"

"Yes, all of them with a single blow."

"The bastards! They should have had their own teeth knocked out so they'd know what it feels like. And these were put in right there at Riga?"

"No way, they were put in while in the Siberian camp."

I did not want to keep Zenta any longer. She was returning from a hard day of laboring so I said, "Well, let's not talk any-more right now. We'll get to it another time."

Zenta asked one more question, "Which section did they put you in?"

"With the disabled ones," I pointed with my arm towards the barrack.

The fourth Latvian Erna introduced at dinner was a tall, middle aged woman, her face totally without expression. Vilma was also in for twenty-five years, and was not interested in nor surprised by anything. She moved like a robot, having completely lost all interest in life and in the outside world.

I could not fall asleep for a long time that night. Heavy thoughts tortured me, especially the difference in response between those who recently arrived in prison and those who already spent a long time behind barbed wire, isolated from the outside world. Within the Riga Cheka or Central Prison, inmates, regardless of paragraph, still show a lively interest in what is happening outside.

Vilma knew that I was from her native country, Latvia. She asked no questions about how things were there, whether Latvian was still spoken. At first I thought that perhaps she did not want to burden me with questions on my first day. But as days, weeks, and months passed I realized that no one sentenced to more than ten years asked a single question about anything. The outside world no longer seemed to exist for them. They had trained themselves not to think. But perhaps that is not the case. Perhaps they only hide their thoughts.

The next day though I did not have to work, I still reported myself present at the morning head count. Sleeping late is not allowed. Another working day starts after the count. Those able to work lined up near the gate leading up to the work zone. The disabled lined up near the other gate, leading to work outside the zone. Soon the Commandant appeared, in the same dirty blouse, and told me I was assigned to the agricultural brigade. During the day I was brought to the warehouse to pick out my black prisoner's garb, a choice between an outfit too small and one too large. I took the oversized one. The boots were large but fit well enough once tightly laced. They were made of bumpy artificial leather and tarpaulin with rubber soles. I found rags to wrap around my feet before putting on the boots so I would not blister my skin.

Impatiently I waited for the end of the working day when I would meet with my new acquaintances. Zenta interested me, and I felt as if I already knew her.

When, after dinner, Zenta came to the bench where I sat and smoked, I asked her, "What did they give you twenty-five years for?"

"Because I was in the forest."

"When did they catch you?"

"1949"

"But then you should have gone home when everyone was released in 1956, during Khruschev's large commission."

"You're right, many returned home. Only a few of us from Latvia were left behind," Zenta said sadly.

"What reason did they give?"

"Nothing, they only said that they could not let us go home yet."

"The other one was Vilma?"

"Yes."

"What was her case?"

"She worked in the passport section of the local township's police department."

"And that was all that was held against her?"

"Yes, there was no alternative in those days. Everybody was given twenty-five years, plus another five without rights. But then those who were released to go home in 1956 received the same sentence."

"How did they decide who remained and who left? Why did they keep you two in particular?"

"Among the women, two with twenty-five year sentences were kept. Many men were retained. They considered each case. If no dead bodies were involved, they were released. Suspicions or proof of dead bodies guaranteed that the commission did not release them."

"If Vilma was working in the passport office, where did the dead bodies come from?"

"The fact that she worked at the government office was part of her trouble."

"And were there dead bodies in your case?"

"There were," she answered quietly.

"Whose were they?"

"I don't know. I never saw any, but on paper they're part of the case. They said that we had to have shot someone while living in the forest. They maintained that our men shot several while we were surrounded and shot at. We didn't even have any ammunition for six months before being surrounded."

"But how did you end up in the forest?"

"I shouldn't have hidden in the forest. I was seventeen and hopelessly in love with a fellow who was twenty. There was no way he could avoid being called up. When the war ended, the older men advised him to take to the woods. Otherwise the Russians would find him and shoot him since he still wore the German uniform."

"You truly loved him, didn't you?"

"Yes, that's why I went with him."

"How long did you live in the forest?"

"A long time . . . four years."

"Wasn't it difficult?"

"Don't ask, I cannot explain it to anyone. Things were the worst in the winter when we had no food. During the summertime we managed."

"But where did you sleep while it was freezing outside?"

"We excavated underground bunkers. With body heat we didn't feel the cold."

"Like animals in their caves."

"That's how it was."

"Where there other women too?"

"At first there were five of us, but one died during the first year. A year later another one died, leaving three of us."

"I can hardly imagine living four years in a cave in the forest, pursued like a frightened animal."

"Several times they threatened to surround us. Once I thought we were trapped, but fortunately we escaped through the marshes."

"They knew that you were in the forest?"

"They knew everything, including the fact that we were unable to escape. They were in no particular hurry to catch us."

"And once they caught you, what happened?"

"They took us to prison and beat us terribly."

"Everybody got twenty-five years?"

"The death sentence for the men; twenty-five years for the two of us. The third woman was wounded so severely after being captured that she died in prison before the trial."

"What happened to the other woman sentenced along with you?"

"She died five years later in the correctional camp. She was past fifty when we were captured, and she was sick."

"And your boyfriend? What happened to him?"

"He got the death sentence, they shot him."

"You're the only survivor of all those who lived in the forest?"

"Yes," Zenta said with a heavy sigh.

"Do you have any relatives?"

"I do, parents and a brother."

"What about them?"

"Nothing in particular, they write and wait for me to come home."

"According to the new penal code, your sentence should be over soon."

"If they lift it." Zenta said with pronounced indifference.

"They have to lift it. If according to the code, the maximum is fifteen years. Nobody can get more than fifteen. After that there's only the death sentence."

"The men who already served more than fifteen had nothing lifted, they were taken out and shot."

"They were taken out and shot, without any sentence?"

"I only know that there was an observation commission which reviewed their cases. They were told their sentences could not be reduced. After a few days they were shot."

"I'm no longer surprised at anything. Are you afraid they won't want to reduce your sentence?"

"Nobody can foretell the future."

"Why don't you write an appeal for parole to Riga?"

"I've never written one."

"I'll be glad to do it for you. It's a real pity that so much time has been lost."

"You really think that it's worthwhile to write it?" Zenta asked shyly, as if she were waking from a hundred year sleep. This change was noticeable during the following days when we tackled the appeal. Several months later the answer came that Zenta was pardoned and could leave the camp.

Vilma's situation was different. She kept to herself, never revealing anything in conversation more than "Good day, how are you?" and then disappearing immediately like a doe. Once safely away, she would find a private corner, usually a wooden staircase to sit on and do her handicrafts. She made embroidered handkerchiefs, one of which she gave me on my name's day (which is the Latvian equivalent of a birthday). She presented it shyly and disappeared immediately. Perhaps she was shy ever since she was a child.

Nina was quite different. She loved people and was always chatting with somebody. One night I sat with her for several hours while she told me about the people in charge of the camp. She was extremely well informed. There was not a single old woman whose life's story, or at least the best part of it, Nina didn't know. In fact her whole appearance proclaimed that she knew it all. Her conclusions were to the point and made sense.

Then one night Nina finally told me about herself: She grew up in hardship. In 1940 when she was a child, her parents were sent to Siberia. Once there, she survived by eating the potato peelings and fish heads she scavenged from garbage cans. She eventually married a Ukrainian and gave birth to a son who was in Riga. She once had a very close and warm-hearted girl-friend whom she trusted, and to whom she revealed her child-hood sufferings and bitter outlook on the Soviet system. But her friend, in turn, told everything to her father. The father turned her in to the Cheka. Nina was given ten years of strict regime in correctional camps. More than nine years were behind her. Despite her suffering, Nina was an optimist. Many people did not like her openness and bluntness. She never flattered or pre-tended, but expressed exactly what she thought of people. I could not help but think well of Nina.

CHAPTER 10

THE LITHUANIANS

Of prisoners from the Baltic republics, the largest share came from Lithuania, then Estonia, and finally from Latvia. The Lithuanian and Estonian women were sentenced mainly for helping the people who, for various reasons at the end of the war, took to the forest.

Most of the Lithuanians worked in the sewing section. Some important people were visiting the camp. They came to inspect the sewing section, but on leaving they asked whether there were complaints. Whoever initiated the question must have regretted it later, for as soon as it was heard above the buzz and racket of the sewing machines the prisoners complained in one voice about the camp shop. Having received no deliveries for over a month, the shop had only envelopes and soap. The visitors, feeling that the situation was out of hand, edged toward the door. However several women deliberately blocked their path and complained loudly. The local administration ordered the women back to their tables and work, and promised that the next day the shop would have everything. It did not; not the next day, nor the day after, nor for the next several weeks.

After this incident a Lithuanian friend of mine, Birute, told me, "You can never trust these bastards who promise everything and deliver nothing. Earlier, when we were in the large camps in Siberia that housed over a thousand inmates, we were fed with promises only. Once we staged an uprising because of lack of food. We couldn't take it any longer. We started with talks. When that didn't help, we threatened not to work. While the administration telephoned for the troops, we collected all the rocks we could find and barricaded ourselves behind beds and mattresses.While the Army fired on us unarmed women, four of us crawled along the roof. Others handed us rocks, which we threw at the soldiers. When the uprising was over two of us climbed down from the roof, the other two were carried off, badly wounded. They both died. Altogether six inmates were killed, and scores were wounded."

"In our zone the administration immediately picks up and pockets any stone that could be sharpened. I've noticed it several times, and could never figure out why. Now it makes sense."

"After uprisings like ours, an order was issued for all camps to pick up stones in the zone. Uprisings still happen, but only in the large camps. They wouldn't dare torture the inmates with hunger in a large camp."

Then I asked, "Why weren't you released after the 1956 Commission? Were there dead bodies in your case?"

"There were, but not in that sense. It was horrible, and I can still see it. I was a student at the Medical Insititute. When the Chekists came to the institute in broad daylight to arrest me in 1950, I had no idea what they were up to. When I was taken into the professor's room, he was lying on the floor, dead. I was only a sophomore and did not understand anything. I couldn't take my eyes off the professor lying on the floor. A narrow trickle of blood curled from the corner of his mouth down his neck, and formed a dark red pool. Suddenly the youngest Chekist leaped on the professor's chest and jumped up and down like an ape. Each jump caused wheezing and roaring sounds to come from the dead man's throat. So many years have passed but I still remember that horrible scene. That was the body in my case."

"What happened afterwards?"

"After the jumping ape finished, I was taken downstairs to a prisoner's van. I don't know if you realize, but in 1956 an inmate's character was extremely important to the commission. The administration of each camp had to prepare character descriptions, so they were forced to use professional traitors to supply information. The main informer in our camp was Masha Saltykova, whose crime was so serious that she had no hope of parole. For that reason she showed no mercy against anyone she didn't like; me for example, because I told her to face that her informing is a big sin. Even now Masha goes into the commandant's room at night to pass information."

"Yes, I was warned during my first week not to say anything about myself to her because everything I said would be known by the commandant the next day. My first day here Masha said that we should get better acquainted. She gave me a whole pack of Sever cigarettes and said there were plenty more where that came from. The same night, as everyone rushed to dinner, I went to the section to get my spoon and ran into Masha who asked me to eat at her place, and joked that I'd have enough time to become familiar with government issue dinners. I was confused and Masha, as though she were an old friend, took me by the hand and led me to her bed. She told me to sit down while she rummaged in her little closet. She took out a loaf of bread, a knife, an opened can of sprats, and a brand new can of salmon. I was really amazed, and she explained that her sister brought her the food. She opened the canned salmon and told me to eat. I finished off the sprats, and had a piece of the salmon. While she was putting away the salmon I went for tea. She served expensive chocolates with the tea. I mentioned that her sister seemed to be making a lot of money. Masha shyly added that she only did it a couple times a year. She didn't ask me anything much, only what I was in for. Please tell me about the spy schools."

"Masha knows what she's doing. She graduated from two spy schools. She finished the first spy school during the war in Leningrad and was sent to Germany where she was captured. Immediately she enrolled in a spy school with the Abwehr—the German intelligence bureau. All of the students were Russian prisoners of war brought together by Canaris. It was a famous spy school even before the war."

"So, she was a double agent. How did Masha trip herself up?"

"When the war ended, she was in Czechoslovakia and returned to her mother's in Leningrad with some made-up story. She married an admiral and everything was fine. Then one night Masha was at the theater with her husband and a former officer recognized her. This officer knew everything, because a Russian prisoner managed to send information on Masha while still in Germany. That's why she couldn't be released by the 1956 Commission."

"How old is she?"

"She's forty-seven. She was already thirty-three when she was arrested. She will certainly be paroled, there's no doubt abut that. She's telling on everybody, from the guards up to the big chiefs. She once turned in a section head who bought a fur coat from an inmate in return for food. The section head disappeared and nobody ever heard from her again."

"Several women told me that any casually dropped remark might be a bonanza, material that can be used against you when it is your turn to be reported on."

From then on, my relationship with Birute was close, and I struck up friendly relations with the other Lithuanians and Estonians as well. One young Lithuanian even gave me a pair of earrings. A gift of earrings in a forced labor camp might sound strange, but she did not expect me to wear them or show them off in camp. She gave me the amber earrings so I would remember her.

A recent arrival, Ona, had graduated from an Institute of Physical Culture and was qualified to teach physical education in high schools. She was strong and volunteered to empty the latrines. No one wanted to do that work, yet to everyone's amazement a young girl with a higher education volunteered to do it. In the civilized world a tanker drives up and pumps the toilets empty. In the camps a small bucket was attached to the end of the long pole for scooping and pouring into a huge vat. A horse pulled the vat when filled to the gate where a trusted inmate took charge of emptying the vat. At six P. M. the inmates's freedom expired and he had to be back inside the zone and behind the barbed wire.

Ona probably knew that what she was doing would preserve her health. Emptying the latrines was done only twice a month, for a day-and-a-half. The rest of the time she was off. She received a monthly bonus of three gallons of milk in addition to the monthly salary of twenty rubles. The milk was issued all at once, straight from the cow. The fresh milk did not keep for more than a day, nor when curdled, did it last for more than four. Naturally she did not finish off the three gallons by herself. Her friends received mugsfull.

One day Ona said, "I hear that you know several foreign languages. For several years I planned to travel. But everything fell apart. Now I'm here for six years. I was working in a Black Sea spa, teaching physical education as part of the therapy. A Russian who works in the Swedish embassy arrived for rest and recuperation. She had a Soviet passport validated for going abroad. I noticed that she looked similar to me. So one morning when most of the guests were on a day-long bus excursion, the embassy-worker included, I went into her bedroom, opened the drawer of her bureau, and pocketed her passport. Within an hour I packed my bag and left the spa without being noticed. A couple of hours later I flew into Moscow and bought my ticket for Sweden, showing the passport. Everything went smoothly since the photo in the passport looked even more like me. Then the weather turned bad in Sweden, and the planes were not flying from Moscow to Stockholm."

"You must have been nervous counting the hours."

"Hours? I was counting the minutes, and then every second." Then Ona announced, with special emphasis, "Exactly six hours, fourteen minutes, and thirty seconds after the scheduled departure, they arrested me. Two young men in dark blue suits approached from two sides simultaneously. They flipped out their badges and rattled off in unison, 'your papers!'"

If the weather had not turned bad in Sweden, Ona would not be emptying the latrines in camp #17-A in Mordovia. As I found out later, in the men's zones this chore was normally carried out by people with higher educations, too. It was an occupation for professionals.

I was introduced to a quiet, retiring Lithuanian, sentenced for nationalism. She was a middle-aged woman, a teacher by profession. She did not speak much and never told anyone about herself. She greeted everybody, however, who crossed her path. The only thing anyone knew about her was that she was allowed to receive letters and small parcels once a year from relatives in the United States containing items such as soap and writing materials. She spent her free time walking back and forth along the fence on one side of the camp, barely keeping the prescribed minimum distance from the barbed wire. She trampled a regular footpath, walking winter and summer, rain or shine.

Another Lithuanian was scheduled to finish her ten-year sentence within a few days. She was deeply affected by this approaching event and felt both excitement and worry about what she would do when free. Leaving confinement was not a happy prospect if one did not have relatives or close friends waiting outside. Being expected and well-received was not as important as having a place to stay. Of equal gravity was the problem of registering one's passport. Returning inmates are not normally accepted for registration. The penalty for living without being registered, if no other crime has been committed, is a return to the camps for two or three years. Since this woman had no relatives to help during this difficult first stage, her anxiety was justified.

While we were discussing who did or did not have relatives, several stories came to light. Another Lithuanian, also in for twenty-five years, watched as a child from a barn loft as a mob of drunken Chekists drove into her family's yard, gathered the entire family of eight, shot them in cold blood and drove off laughing. The young girl, speechless with fear from witnessing the shooting of her parents, grandparents, brothers, and sisters, left everything and hid in the forest. She stayed in the forest alone, without food for several days.

After several days passed, she met some compatriots she knew. She lived with them until the Cheka and the Army surrounded the forest. Everyone living in the forest was arrested and automatically given twenty-five years, without question. Had the Cheka known she was a witness to their atrocities, they would have shot her without a trial. By remaining silent about her true reasons for being in the forest, the girl survived.

By the time I met her she was a middle-aged woman, her legs still badly scarred from the bullets received while the forest was encircled. She lived without joy, without her family. She had no hopes. The future no longer existed for her, only the past and the present. The most characteristic thing about her was the fact that she never spoke about her past or her lost family. The only ones who knew about her grim life were a few Lithuanian women to whom, during her first years of imprisonment, she talked about herself.

Some Estonians never spoke about their experiences, saying that their suffering was too heavy for them to discuss. Also, everyone had personal sorrows and problems, which were enough in themselves without hearing others speak of the pains that had wrecked their lives and the tortures that they had passed through. By telling others about their sufferings, they only relived the experiences without feeling better or easing their mind.

In a way they were right. On the other hand, if no one ever spoke others would never learn of the Cheka's cruelty. Try as the Cheka might to hide and suppress these blotches on its honor, to change events that had taken place, or to even deny that they had occurred, they will never succeed, as long as the victims talk about them, write about them, and keep them in their memories.

CHAPTER 11

ESPECIALLY DANGEROUS STATE CRIMINALS

I was impatient to know what crimes brought so many women to a strict regime camp. During my first days in camp, Nina explained that about seventy-five percent of the women were there because of religious practices, and only twenty-five percent were sentenced for political motives. Most of the political inmates were peasant women from Ukraine. Some of them along with their men were found hiding in the forest when the war ended. Others were sentenced for giving bread and milk to their compatriots in the forest. One day a Ukrainian peasant woman said "I believe you know how to write. Couldn't you write a piece of paper for me so that they'd reduce my sentence?"

Her pleading eyes would not leave mine and I promised to put together her plea within the next day or two. Her situation was simple. She lived alone, close to the forest. She kept a cow. The men hiding in the forest threatened to shoot her unless she gave them milk or bread. Her neighbor observed the nightly visits and turned her in to the militia. She received twenty-five years of confinement in a penal camp.

Another time I spoke with a young Ukrainian girl called Nastenka. Barely able to read and write, she delivered a case of political flyers to Odessa. For that she received ten years. I wrote Nastenka a petition for parole since nothing else could help her. Three months later the news came that Nastenka was being paroled. Overjoyed, she left me a small soft cushion as a memento. Later a letter came form Odessa, explaining that she was working as a dishwasher in a canteen, and was allowed to eat as much as she wanted. Nastenka's handwriting and style were like a child's. Everybody was amazed at Nastenka's parole, having taken it for granted that nobody could go home before serving her entire sentence.

A few days later after Nastenka left, I met a new "friend," Jurisson. She was an older Estonian with an unholy character. She did not have to work and ran through the zone, cursing everybody she met. She suspected people of stealing everything: Her soap, her towel, her bedsheet from the clothesline. In the evening however the bedsheet was on her bed, she hadn't remembered that she'd carried it inside herself. Her preferred sitting spot was the little bench near the gates where she could see who was coming and who was going. Whenever somebody high in the administration arrived, she would run to him, grab his sleeve with both hands and rattle off complaints against the other inmates. One of them spilled soup on her, someone else stole her shirt, and once again, her soap was stolen. When the administration tried to get rid of her by promising to investigate the matters, Jurisson simply switched to a different topic. According to her, nobody in the entire zone could be trusted; everybody lied and acted under false pretenses. This went on endlessly.

All the officials ran from Jurisson. And now she wanted to make friends with me. Wherever I went there she was, waiting. She showered me with gifts, a yellow enameled mug for tea, then an old beaten aluminum bowl. Only several weeks later did she explain her sudden friendship: She too needed a plea for parole.

Putting the plea together was not easy because Jurisson refused to admit to the crime for which she was sentenced. She recounted only an approximate version of what occurred. Her neighbors were always stealing from her. When she unmasked them, they turned her over to the militia, swearing under oath that Jurisson prayed to God both by herself and with others in her room at night. Their libelous testimony brought Jurisson a ten-year sentence. She wanted me to write that in her plea. In vain I explained that first she had to admit guilt because the gist of the case was that she insulted her neighbors by calling them thieves. It took me several weeks to convince Jurisson how the plea should be worded if she wanted to go home.

The entire zone commiserated over my spending hours each day with Jurrison. Finally, the plea was written and mailed. I endured her company for another seven months until the answer arrived. Jurrison was granted parole. She packed her belongings and left so quickly that she never thanked me. But several dozen other inmates gratefully shook my hand to thank me for saving the camp from Jurisson's presence.

Once I overheard a brief conversation which stuck in my memory. In the camp where the inmates received twenty-five year sentences for political causes, the actual level of political knowledge was low. Two old women, one Lithuania, one Ukrainian, were speaking Russian. The Lithuanian waved her walking stick at a photo of Lenin on the wall, saying: "See, that's Lenin that they've hung on the wall there. Must be a clever man. D'you know if he's still alive?" (This was 1965.) The Ukrainian, sneaking a look at her partner, muttered to herself, "You old stupid bag," and announced aloud that he had been dead for ages.

Why did they keep these old women imprisoned? None of them were physically capable of doing any work, nor could anyone receive any benefit from them.

One more political inmate left the camp before completing her sentence. Valentina Semyonovna Sanagina was well past seventy. Her lawyer friend, Skripnikova, helped to prepare her pleas from outside the camp. Sanagina's political crime was unique. In her old age she decided to write a book about her life, starting with her childhood. Before she was finished, the Cheka ransacked her home, confiscated the half-finished book, and arrested her. Her manuscript recorded her childhood memories of her despotic father, who in drunken stupors beat his wife and children. However this despot was a member of the Communist party. For slandering a Party member, Sanagina was awarded ten years in a strict regime correction camp. Sanagina spent eight years before she gained a new hearing, which reduced her sentence. In the eyes of the Cheka, Sanagina commited a dangerous political crime. She was sentenced in 1958 when everybody believed the terror of Stalin's era was over. However the Cheka continued to work according to the proven pattern.

Anna Aleksandrovna Borkova was born in 1890. A revolutionary, journalist by profession, working in the Kremlin as the First Commissar for Culture, Lunacharsky's secretary, she knew Lenin. Despite having devoted her life to Communism, she was in for her third decade.

She was a tiny, extremely thin woman. Her thick white hair, loose to her shoulders, normally blew in the breeze. Because of the wind-blown hair, her narrow face looked even narrower. Her face was covered with freckles and her eyes were unusually small, like two tiny, dark brown pearls darting rapidly to and fro while she read. Borkova never used glasses. No one disturbed or pestered her with small talk and gossip, but kept instead a respectful distance.

I obtained a couple of cigarettes, and offered her one. Anna Aleksandrovna thawed a bit after taking one and asked me to sit down next to her. We sat and talked; Borkova found out all about me, because she shot questions so rapidly all I could do was answer. She decided I had been wronged by the system when I received such a lengthy sentence for reading foreign magazines. A few days later she showed me her photo album. Only later did it dawn on me that this album was her only valuable possession. She had never owned anything besides the album. She didn't own her clothes which were state issue. In prison she wore prisoner's garb, and during her post-revolutionary years in the Kremlin, the state provided everybody with one set of clothes every couple of years. Whenever she was paroled and released from a prison or camp, she was clothed by the state. She never owned a plate or a spoon, let alone furniture or other worldly goods.

As a young woman, finished with her studies, Borkova lived and worked within the Kremlin. During those early days, none of the revolutionaries owned personal possessions because they lived public lives. Reminiscing Borkova said: "The healthiest period of Soviet power was the revolutionary period when we truly were one for all and all for one.

While turning the album's pages, she came to a photo of Lunacharsky, and next to it one of herself as a young woman, seated in the midst of Lunacharsky's family. After closing the album she added, "I've only made one mistake in my life. When Lenin died, I should have shot myself." Strong words, I thought.

I discovered that Borkova was an idealist. She earned her first ten year sentence when, as a journalist, she tried to publish an article about the extravagant lifestyle of Stalin and the members of the Politburo. She wanted to remind everyone that in a communist society it is not permissible for the highest functionaries of the Party to put their personal interests above those of the people. She was sentenced to ten years in prison in 1937, the darkest year in the history of Russia when Stalin shot the most trustworthy idealists in the Communist party.

After spending ten years in prison, Borkova saw that the conditions she criticized had deteriorated. All the Party functionaries had cars and drivers, access to special shops with better quality goods, as well as numerous other privileges. In righteous indignation, Borkova wrote scathingly that the Party was not following the principles of Lenin. Borkova again received ten years in a forced labor camp. After spending six years in the camp, Borkova was released and rehabilitated in 1953, when Stalin died.

Borkova carefully observed the new leadership under Khrushchev, who criticized Stalin. The time arrived, she thought, when the life and work of the high Party officials would be controlled. However, the entire Party and government officials lived in full comfort. Everybody had dachas (villas), servants, cars, and personal chauffeurs. Once again Borkova dared to criticize the highest circles of the Kremlin. For the third time, she received ten years in a correctional camp, regardless of the fact that she already served two terms and had been rehabilitated.

She believed that her sharp critiques would reform the Party and the government. The Cheka on the other hand believed that lengthy sentences would change Borkova. Neither side achieved success. Borkova, smoking cheap tobacco wrapped in strips of newspaper, sat on her bench in camp, still criticizing the government.

Then, Khruschev was out and Borkova was released after seven-and-a-half years, a total imprisonment of twenty-three-and-a-half years. The authorities placed her in the Communist party's old comrades' home, and gave her a personal pension, granted only to Party members. Thus this idealist passed her entire life without a bed, table, or chair that she could call her own.

In the camp were two former members of the Communist Youth movement (Comsomol). One young girl received one year because she once muttered something unacceptable at a Youth meeting. She could no longer recall what she said. The other Communist Youth was a twenty-six year old woman from Georgia, sentenced to two years. During Khrushchev's years, she ran afoul of the anti-Soviet agitation paragraph, applied to the glorification of Stalin. At a Communist Youth meeting she openly defended Stalin after someone criticized him. Stalin could not be called an anti-Soviet element. Therefore defending Stalin could not be interpreted as anti-Soviet action. But apparently the Soviet system had not yet determined how to deal with cases like hers. I once asked the Georgian, "Why did you defend Stalin? Do you know what he was like?"

She replied, "When I was little, they taught us in kindergarten that our most loving father was Stalin. When I later went to school, we were taught that Stalin was the apple of our eye and the bringer of our luck. In the Communist Youth meetings, we were taught that we must be grateful to Stalin for everything and that he was the only true embodiment of the people's wishes. How could I speak otherwise?"

There were a few more inmates among the "particularly dangerous to the state" offenders, whose crimes were unusual and worthy of mention. One was a student from Moscow University. She was part of a group interested in learning more than what was offered in the official course program. One enterprising youth discovered a library hidden in the attic of the university building and was able to make a duplicate key. Only a small circle of friends knew about the secret library, among them this girl. With great precautions, they visited the library to read the forbidden authors like Freud, Kant, Lessing, and others.

Despite their precautions, other students followed and betrayed them. All of them were arrested and sentenced to five years in a strict regime forced labor camp for anti-Soviet agitation. The student who initiated the crime and under whose influence the others joined, received seven years. Is there any other country where reading Freud will earn a prison sentence?

The case of Tamara was also strange. A Russian, she was living in the Ukraine. Tamara's brother-in-law regularly listened to the "Voice of America" and "Radio Liberty." He interested Tamara and both of them listened. There was an extreme food shortage in their provincial town which lacked butter, other dairy products and meat for months. When somebody at work complained about not having enough to eat, Tamara and her brother-in-law told them what they heard on the radio:

Some people had enough food and some to spare. The Cheka arrested them for spreading lies. The court handed down a "just" verdict of guilt for denigration of the true living conditions in Russia and spreading the false foreign propaganda. Tamara received three years, but her older brother-in-law received five.

Another case involved Esperanto. Although not a popular language in the Soviet Union, some study it. There is even an Esperanto Club. One club member received permission to visit the Esperanto fans in Bulgaria. She struck up friendships and corresponded in Esperanto. Within a short time one of her letters to Bulgaria "accidently" reached the Cheka. Not pleased with the contents of the letter, the Cheka decided to teach this club member a lesson. They arrested her and gave her three years for denigration of the true conditions of Soviet life.

A woman doctor in Minsk, Byelorussia, who lived with her entire family in a damp narrow basement apartment was unhappy with her living conditions. She wrote to President Kennedy, apparently expecting that her case would be talked about abroad, and that the Russians would be shamed into giving her a more suitable apartment. But the letter went directly from the mailbox to the Cheka. Her writing to Kennedy and denigrating the true conditions of Soviet life earned her five years in a strict regime corrective labor camp.

There was another "particularly dangerous criminal against the state" whose crime made everyone grin. Despite being a cook at a big restaurant she was denied an apartment. Angry with the Party and Khrushchev's government, she drew a corn cob on a strategic spot of Khrushchev's picture on the front page of a magazine. For this, she was given three years.

Nobody knew what Tanya was sentenced for. She seemed rather stupid and nobody could understand her stories. She walked around singing to herself. When I first saw her she was pregnant. During her final two months she did not have to work and received supplementary food rations: half a glass of milk, one egg, and a knife tip of butter daily. Her child was born in the hospital, located several hours drive from camp #17-A. The child died and Tanya was brought back.

If the child had lived, Tanya would have remained at the hospital and received supplementary rations for another six months, although even breastfeeding mothers in the hospital

*Especially Dangerous
State Criminal*

worked. During the first six months a mother fed her baby. The baby would be taken from her the first day she ran out of milk and handed over to the children's home while the mother would be returned to prison. Once she completed her sentence, the mother could claim her baby. If she did not want the child, however, she would not have to claim it.

Tanya returned to the camp and after a few months sharp eyes noticed that she was about to have another child. The women talked about her, "She isn't too bright, but apparently she's got enough brains to know how to make children." Once again Tanya received the extra rations for expectant mothers, did not work, and walked around the camp, singing. What Tanya was in for no one ever learned.

To prevent camp life from becoming too monotonous and so that inmates would not think too much about their personal problems, artistic and cultural activities were encouraged. The camps held folk dance competitions and the best troupes traveled for guest performances to other camps. Most camps had a choir and various quartets and soloist singers.

Camp #17-A however, had neither dancers nor singers and instead, literary evenings became popular. During these evenings an inmate read either a poem or a prose work. The choice of authors was restricted to the classical Russian writers such as Gogol, Pushkin, and Lermontov. Dora Borisovna led these literary evenings. A professional literature teacher, she worked in Russian high schools until her retirement.

Once retired, Dora Borisovna submitted a proposal to the government comparing the Hebrew culture with other U.S.S.R. cultures. She noted the fact that other cultures have their own publishers, their own movie studios and theaters, and are allowed to stage cultural weeks in Moscow to demonstrate singing, dancing, performing arts and folk arts. Dora Borisovna noted that in a country as international as the U.S.S.R., where friendship between and equality of culture is constantly proclaimed, Hebrew is the only culture unable to cultivate and display its folk traditions and cultural riches.

The Soviet Ministry of Culture, instead of answering directly, handed the case over to the Cheka which decided to punish Dora Borisnova and her husband with seven years each in strict regime corrective labor camps, basing their sentence on the paragraph on nationalism. Dora Borisovna was nearsighted, so could not take part in corrective labor. As a woman who actively worked her whole life, she took the lead in organizing the literary evenings. These evenings were beneficial because many of the inmates in the camp, sentenced on political grounds, had not completed their education.

All Soviet penal settlements have schools to serve the young criminals. For them the prison school was obligatory. Camp #17-A had no school because the average age of the inmates was fifty. However one inmate, Vera, insisted on learning. At twenty-four she wanted to finish primary school. She was allowed to study on her own and twice a year was mailed a list of printed test questions to be answered in writing. The entire camp helped her to prepare for her examinations.

Vera could not explain what exactly she was accused of. She said they talked at a furious pace in court, rattling off the numbers of the applicable penal code paragraphs. However she could not recall what she was charged with. This factor probably influenced her desire to complete her education by reading in camp.

CHAPTER 12

JEHOVAH'S WITNESSES

After living with the inmates of the penal camp, I realized how few were in for political reasons. Most of the women were in the camp for religious "crimes." The Constitution states that there is freedom of religion in the Soviet Union, a half-truth which applies only to the large churches. In the main churches there is usually an official pastor, whose sermons are subject to state censorship. He is permitted to express from the pulpit only state-approved views. For example, on June 14, 1941 Stalin began the first wave of massive deportations of Latvians. In the free world this day is observed as a national day of mourning. If a pastor in Latvia were to mention these deportations during a sermon, he would be sentenced for "distortion of Soviet reality." After serving his sentence he could labor at a collective farm, but he would never again be allowed onto the pulpit.

One of the most persecuted religious groups in the Soviet Union is the Jehovah's Witnesses most of whom live in the former Romanian territory of Moldavia in the Ukraine and in the Irkutsk region of Siberia. Founded in 1872 by Charles Taze Russell in Pittsburgh, the Jehovah's Witnesses are headquartered in Brooklyn, New York. The Soviet Jehovah's Witnesses receive their religious literature from Brooklyn illegally since its importation into the Soviet Union is strictly forbidden. In fact, literature from Brooklyn arrives regularly, in good shape and in large quantities through unofficial and well-organized channels, not only in many cities, including Siberia, but even in the penal camps of Potma. This fact distressed the camp authorities. No one could understand how this land of barbed wire and limited human contact could be penetrated by forbidden literature—and from the United States at that!

Many Jehovah's Witnesses receive ten years of hard labor merely for having a few issues of the magazine *Watchtower* in their apartments. Since people are arrested for possession of

125

these writings, the anxiety and exasperation of the administration over the presence of this literature in camp is understandable. No one has discovered how it gets into the camp. After all, following conviction, every prisoner is stripped of all clothing and completely searched. On arrival at the camp each prisoner is thoroughly searched again, down to the last seam. Suitcases are searched for double bottoms. No stranger is allowed into the camp without good cause. When inmates are let out of the camp zone for work in the fields, they are surrounded by armed guards and no one is permitted to approach them. A thorough search of each prisoner is made when they return to the camp in the evening. But despite this surveillance, the Brooklyn literature finds its readers.

In the camp the Jehovah's Witnesses were the most disadvantaged because they were under constant surveillance. If more than three of them gathered, they were ordered to disperse. The camp authorities maintained a list of festivals honored by each religion. On one Jehovah's Witnesses holiday armed soldiers were brought in and positioned nearby to wait for the services to begin. Their services began with singing hymns outdoors. Previously organized, the women gathered rapidly, one gave the pitch, and all began to sing. Before the hymn was finished, the camp gates opened and the soldiers and the camp director marched in. The director approached the singing women and ordered them to disperse. They ignored her and continued to sing. Then the director raised her voice and shouted, "I order you to disperse!" No results. "Whom am I ordering?" Still no reaction. The Jehovah's Witnesses sang louder. Then the camp director went up to the head of the soldiers and spoke with him quietly; she shrugged and returned to the women. "I am warning you for the last time, get moving at once. You are breaking camp regulation. You know singing is not allowed in the camp." No response. The camp director stood helplessly and listened.

The women disregarded the director, finished one hymn, and started another. The director could hardly contain herself, bit her lip, and darted infuriated looks. "I will give orders to shoot," she threatened. No reaction came from the women, who looked entranced, even blissful, standing close to each other singing. I decided that the soldiers armed with machine guns were present merely to intimidate the women. If the order to shoot came, it would be to shoot above their heads. But that did not happen. When the women finished singing their three hymns, they left without even glancing at the director, as if nothing had happened.

The Jehovah's Witnesses were mainly young women with a few older ones serving second sentences. First sentences ranged from five to seven years, while second sentences were ten years. All Jehovah's Witnesses, except for the Group II disabled, worked at all camp jobs, mainly in the serving division.

After work, during rest periods, they regularly recited Bible verses. The more capable ones also studied foreign languages— French, English, and German—in order to translate the religious literature for those who did not understand. It was because of the Jehovah's Witnesses that the camp was so frequently searched. No matter how carefully they hid their scraps of paper with biblical quotations and excerpts from their translations, the authorities always found something.

Often, especially after dark, guards loitered outside the windows to observe what the Jehovah's Witnesses were doing in their beds. If they noticed anyone writing or reading from a scrap of paper, the guards rushed in to tear the paper from the girl's grasp. Often they found only a letter to a relative.

Several times a year the authorities carried out what were known as major raids. Although they always took place on Sundays, no one could predict them. I recall one typical raid when the guards burst through the gates, ran into the various sections and barred all the exits. "With bedding to the work zone!" they ordered. Everyone, ill or well, picked up her bedding and moved. By the gate the women guards shook all the sheets one by one and searched pockets and bodies from head to foot. When the body searches were completed, all inmates were herded into the work zone. Each put down her bedding, sat on it and waited. Conversations were strained. As soon as all the inmates were in the work zone, the camp was thoroughly searched, often for several hours.

After the search was over, the inmates were allowed to return and tidy up the sleeping area. Once after such a search, the camp director called me into her office. I was surprised, knowing that no clandestine papers were among my things. The director, Anna Aleksejevna, spread five issues of *Watchtower* before me. They were written in different languages, but

After the search was over, all were allowed to return.

the director, although a teacher by training, did not recognize the languages. I had never seen the magazine and wanted to read, which I knew would not be allowed. Therefore, I said, "All right. Let me look closely at the spelling. You know, the European languages are so much alike that I could make a mistake. And I want to be accurate." While I was speaking, I had already read a few sentences in the German copy. One verse stuck in my memory: "Be harmless as a dove and wise as a serpent." I have often thought about this sentence which is not bad advice for people who have to survive in the Soviet Union.

When I stopped reading because the director was becoming suspicious, I placed the magazines into three piles and declared, "These two are in English, those two are in French, and this one is in German." The director was delighted, since she could mention the languages of the confiscated magazines in her report. The magazines had been found buried in the flower beds, but how they had come into the camp zone, no one knew.

One day while working in the field I could not stand up. I felt such sharp pain in my spine that I could not move. The guard was notified, he passed the message on to the mobile guards, and by the time the work day ended, a horse and a cart arrived. The Jehovah's Witnesses gently lifted me into the cart, lifted me out at the gate and carried me inside the zone, into my barracks and placed me in my bed. All through my sickness they were diligent nurses. I could not have wished for better care, especially under camp conditions. Every one of them should have studied medicine and worked with the seriously ill in hospitals. The severe shortage of nursing personnel in the Soviet Union amounts to an emergency. The wages are so low that it is only possible to recruit chronic alcoholics who are not tolerated anywhere else. Consequently, patients in hospitals receive practically no nursing care.

Jehovah's Witnesses consider it their duty to help everyone, regardless of religion or nationality. As no one ever nursed and pampered me like these young women, I found it almost difficult to accept. While nursing me, they sat at my bedside for hours trying to convert me. Although I said that I had been christened and had my own faith, they explained that it was their duty to share theirs. In contrast to the rest of the inmates, I was more patient, and was interested in hearing their proselytization. Considering their educational level, they knew their subject well and knew many Bible verses by heart.

> One woman who had been a member for four years was struggling. She explained, "I lost my house in a fire, and my two children died. I had a difficult time. Then the sisters consoled me and preached their faith. I accepted and two years later I was arrested. Now God is testing my faith."

I asked, "And you don't regret having accepted the faith for which you now must sit in prison?"

"What can be done? Everything happens according to God's will. If we must suffer here, that is because of our sins," she sighed.

I continued, "I do not think the Soviet labor camps are for penance; they are punitive camps where the Party puts people for thinking differently from the government. All of you are in prison not because you believe, but because you preach and try to convert. If you sat at home alone and prayed quietly to God, no one would ever find out or take you to court."

"That is true, But it is our duty to preach and gain new brothers and sisters. We should not be so egotistical to prepare only ourselves for the millennium on earth. All people should be informed so they can live in it. If someone refuses, that is their own business."

Several of the Jehovah's Witnesses told me about events that occurred in connection with their faith. I wondered where they found the strength and energy to carry out such risky and complicated activities. For example, a clandestine printing press was discovered in Irkutsk where translated literature was printed in Russian, in order to reach greater masses of people.

One of the women volunteered, "I don't tell anyone that I speak German. I know you do and we could talk to each other in German."

"Fine. In fact I prefer German to Russian."

"Did you know I was in Germany," she asked.

I was not particularly surprised, as several people had been to Germany. To continue the conversation I asked, "Long ago?"

"It was about ten years ago, when I went to the Netherlands to attend the international conference of the Jehovah's Witnesses."

"Really? But where did you get the necessary documents for the trip?"

"You think I traveled with documents? Without documents! I crossed the border on foot and traveled to Holland. I returned on foot. Besides, I had a large pile of literature to carry back." I looked at her in disbelief. "What do you say to that?" she asked after seeing my astonishment.

"And you went alone?"

"I went alone, but God was with me everywhere."

"But that's incredible!"

"It sounds unbelievable, but it happened, not once, but twice!"

"Both times without documents?"

"Yes. Both times on foot across the border and back."

"If that's true, then God must have guided you across the border."

"Yes, my dear, such is God's power. To make the visible invisible, to make the audible inaudible, and much more."

"But power in your faith is enormous. Without faith, you would never have dared to take such a risk."

"Without a doubt, that too," she agreed.

I remember, too, another conversation I had with the Jehovah's Witnesses about the gods. They insisted that there were two gods, Jehovah and another, whom Jehovah would fight. No matter how hard they tried, using modern science, chemistry, and the newest findings in physics, they could not prove the existence of the other god to me. Despite our disagreement, I found these women, with a few exceptions, good, charitable, virtuous, and extraordinarily strong in their faith.

Then the Jehovah's Witnesses were suddenly and unexpectedly assailed by the tempter, the devil. The Cheka discovered a new method, never before tried, whereby they hoped to eradicate the Jehovah's Witnesses: by discovering their leaders. The task was difficult, but not impossible. One by one these leaders were taken to Saransk, the capital of Mordovia. Like any larger city, Saransk had stores, theaters, and other attractions. Two Chekists would take a woman, half-starved for years in hard labor camps, to a grocery or restaurant and tell her, "Choose whatever you like. We will buy it for you." When the woman proudly refused, saying that she did not need anything, she was taken to a department store and again offered anything. "Then they would say, "Since you do not want anything, at least have some ice cream," which would be brought to her. The woman would reply, "Thank you. I don't eat ice cream," and would not accept it. "Perhaps you would like to see a movie or a play?" the Chekist would offer, showing his ignorance, because Jehovah's Witnesses never attended the movies that were occasionally brought to the camp and shown to the inmates in the dining room. The woman was kept for a few weeks in the Saransk Cheka where they tried to convince her to leave the group, with the promise of immediate release from prison. When the Chekists accepted their failure, the victim was returned to camp. After a while another one was taken away.

Upon returning to camp, everyone told the same story. It was horrible to tempt people who had already suffered such a long time. To show people, who haven't eaten well for years, shelves of fresh bread, cakes, cookies and other goodies, is actually torture. Only one woman, a young Moldavian, did succumb. No one ever found out exactly how it happened as she never told anyone. Like the others, she was suddenly taken away with her belongings. Before she left, the other women told her what to expect and gave her sound advice. Even so, the young Moldavian was unexpectedly released, despite a remaining five year sentence. Perhaps she wanted to live and could not endure. Possibly she was taken home from which it was impossible to leave. Nevertheless, if she was free to go home, she had also been forced to renounce her faith and to promise in writing and on tape never to return to her religion.

After about half a year this same woman reappeared in the camp, recuperated, well fed, and accompanied by two Chekists. She came not as an inmate, but as a lecturer. She wore a cherry-colored woolen suit, in bad taste but expensive, black patent leather shoes and a matching handbag. The Jehovah's Witnesses were visibly upset. Work in the sewing division stopped and everyone was called to the living section. There, sitting at the head of the table, the former sister delivered a lecture.

She explained that when she accepted the faith she was not aware of what she was doing. She regretted having convinced women in the Moldavian villages of the existence of Jehovah. She regretted having been responsible for ruining so many families. Convinced of her error, she now felt it her duty to lead her former sisters back to real life. She lectured for several hours. She cried. Yet her former sisters viewed her with scorn.

This experience was both upsetting and depressing. That afternoon no one in the camp laughed. Everyone was involved in her own thoughts. No matter how they tried to conceal their feelings, the Jehovah's Witnesses were terribly concerned. I wondered why this display was necessary. Was anything gained by it? It was an empty performance for which the administration could draw a check mark on their calendar to indicate that their regular hounding of the religious inmates had been performed. Perhaps the Chekists thought it ingenious; perhaps they imagined that the women would line up to denounce their faith. However, the Chekists achieved the opposite effect.

At that time one Jehovah's Witness began to study the laws from the Criminal code and wrote to the All-Soviet Prosecutor's office. After months of study she had discovered that all of them were tried incorrectly for "agitation against the state." Thus their highest penalty could not exceed three years. As soon as the women heard this, they wrote to the courts that they received seven and ten instead of the three years. One's unnecessary years in prison became the only topic of discussion. One woman spent six extra years. In three or four months every sister who wrote to the court was informed that her penalty, reclassified according to a different section of the law, was now reduced to three years. All of them had already spent four or more years in prison. No one offered compensation for the surplus years, no one apologized or asked forgiveness.

It is difficult to imagine another country where the courts could make such an enormous mistake. Because of the misapplication of the clause, hundreds of people were imprisoned for seven and ten years (with another ten years for second offenders), instead of for three years. Women were serving their second decade for nothing but their faith! Within a year, camp # 17-A had no more Jehovah's Witnesses inmates.

Since they could no longer be classified as "particularly dangerous state criminals," but as ordinary social criminals, Jehovah's Witnesses were placed in camps for criminals. Physically, life was easier for them. Living conditions and food were better. However morally their lives were more difficult because they quickly became objects of ridicule and entertainment for some inmates. At the same time, they continued to proselytize and discovered other inmates ready to accept their faith. There is one tragic footnote to this story: All the Jehovah's Witnesses were released, except one. Because she almost completed her second ten-year term, there was no reason to write. She did not finish serving her time, though, because she died exactly ten days before her release. Agitated, she counted the days until freedom when she would again be among her relatives. The excitement was too much for her heart. In contrast to the women who walked out through the gate, this one was carried out in a coffin made of crude boards. No one knows where she was buried. No matter how hard relatives try, bodies are not released to them.

CHAPTER 13

THE TRUE ORTHODOX

A large proportion of the prisoners, all Russians, were of the sect known as the True Orthodox. Because they wore the traditional garb of nuns, the whole zone called them "the nuns." The rules stated that prison apparel must be black. Theirs was, and anyone who tried to make them change into prison uniforms gave up because the nuns refused. For several months after their imprisonment, the nuns steadfastly refused to wash. Other prisoners were ordered to wrap them in blankets and bring them to the bath house. Once there, the nuns refused to undress. After being forcibly undressed and splashed with water, they quickly dressed and fled to their beds, a sort of refuge or asylum. Eventually the nuns were persuaded that it would not be a sin to go to the bath once every ten days.

The nuns differed from the other prisoners in refusing to work. For their refusal, they were confined innumerable times to the hard punishment cells. According to the law, they could be kept in those cells for three months. Thereafter the local court would arrive, hold a session, and sentence all those whom doctors considered healthy and capable to work.

There is only one place in the Soviet Union for especially dangerous criminals against the state, the Vladimir prison. No matter where the criminal was born or raised, if he or she has been tried for especially dangerous crimes against the state and if the sentence is to be served in prison rather than in a labor camp, the prisoner is sent to Vladimir prison. "Corrective labor camp" means that one must work rather than idly serve one's sentence. Vladimir prison is the only place where one can serve one's time without working, in a locked cell, with the right to a thirty-minute walk once every twenty-four hours. Other strictures include the limit of one letter per month to relatives and a minimum ration of food.

When prisoners were brought from the Vladimir prison,

they looked as though they had been dug from a grave. Their faces were emaciated, unnaturally grayish and pale with sunken eyes. A group of nuns arriving from Vladimir was a terrible sight. Zenta explained that they were from our camp originally.

"There is always someone from our camp in Vladimir prison," she told me.

"For a long time?"

"Usually for three years. At the end of that time, they are returned, and another group is taken there."

"But that is dreadful. Look at them, they look dead!"

"What can you do if their God doesn't allow them to work? We all work, even though it is hard. Sometimes I think I will rebel and refuse to work too. But I can never muster up the courage."

"But on the outside they must have worked."

"They never worked officially," Zenta explained. "None of them ever carried a Soviet passport. They don't touch money, and they don't go to work."

"How can they get by without passports?"

"They never let themselves be photographed, so that's why they don't have passports. The other reason they would never even hold a passport in their hands is because it carries the sign of satan: the five pointed star and the hammer and sickle. The sign of satan is also the reason they do not touch money. And they never go to the doctor; they treat themselves."

"But what if it's serious?"

"Doesn't make any difference. They pick some herbs in the zone. They absolutely refuse to go to the doctor or touch medicine from the dispensary. In Siberia we had several cases where we had to try to save a life. We held their arms and legs down while the nurse gave injections. And what do you think we got for it? The other nuns heaped the world's worst curses upon us. Then they tried to hide their illnesses until several died. To this day they believe that doctors and medicine come from satan, only they themselves are good. I can tell you, they come from satan too," Zenta concluded angrily.

"I'd like to know how the court can sentence these women to three years in Vladimir prison when they don't know the state of their health."

"This idiocy of theirs is to blame. If they went to the doctor, only a few would be declared capable of labor. The rest would officially be declared invalids."

"You know, they don't seem too bright. Even without a doctor or any medical tests, it's clear that some of them are quite ill."

"Sure they're ill, everybody knows that. But a doctor's certificate is essential. He's the only one who can release anybody from work."

"This thing about not touching money. Here in prison no one has any, but how do they survive outside, pay for rent, transportation, food?"

"They don't live in rented apartments but spend the night wherever they happen to be, usually with the people they do house work for in exchange for food. And if someone gives them an old piece of black clothing they alter it. They don't need transportation because they walk everywhere."

"I still don't understand. How can anyone walk such long distances, say several thousand kilometers?"

"They don't need to go that far."

"What do you mean they don't? Say if one of them has finished serving her sentence and wants to return to her relatives to live where she was living before, will she walk?"

"No. The camp administration will send someone with her to the railroad station to buy her ticket. Then he will give the ticket to the supervisor of the train and put the nun herself into her carriage."

"All right, I understand it so far. She may be on the train several days. How will she eat without money?"

"She will beg her bread from the other travelers. They have no demands beyond bread because they know nothing of secular life. Their shirts are made from rough canvas. I saw one of them completely baffled by brassieres drying on a line. She pointed with her finger and asked: 'What's that thing and what do you do with it?' And another middle-aged nun didn't even know that you can bring berries home from the woods, add sugar and make jam for the winter. When she was told about it, she shook her head in wonder because all her life she went to the woods to eat berries. They think about nothing except God."

I made friends with the nuns from the Tashkent convent. All the nuns, including their "matushka" (abbess), were arrested. Matushka Gorbashova was well along in years. The rest of the nuns respected her and brought her everything she needed. They made her bed, did her laundry, took care of her as well as possible in the camp.

Closest to the matushka were her two assistants, her main counselors. The first one, who appeared to be her closest counselor, had an advanced medical education. Those who knew she graduated from a medical faculty in Soviet Russia but refused all medicine were astounded. The other studied history and was generally intelligent and an interesting conversationalist. All the other nuns were literally servants of God and of this trinity, centered on matushka. The faith of these nuns without education, and from peasant backgrounds, bordered on fanaticism.

Matushka Gorbashova was the oldest, the two educated advisers next, and the rest of varying ages. It was difficult to determine their ages, for their faces were almost invisible, hidden by a head covering different from that worn by ordinary nuns. These headdresses, specially sewn of black cotton, fit the head as closely as a diver's helmet. Only the eyes, nose, and mouth were visible; the rest of the face, eyebrows and half of the cheeks were covered with black fabric. It tied around the neck, and widened around the shoulders to form a capelet ending at the shoulders. The dress was long, down to the ground, and voluminous. Though they all looked alike, one recognized the youngest by her gait. When she thought no one was watching this young nun sometimes pranced like a young doe, her skirt aflutter. Her name was Nadja. Because of her slight build she looked like a high school girl, and I thought her to be eighteen at the most, but she was twenty-one.

Camp life was especially difficult for Nadja, who was brought up in a religious family. Her father was a Bulgarian, her mother a Russian, and the family lived in Tashkent. Along with the other school children, Nadja joined the Pioneers, from which one is automatically promoted to Comsomol. When her parents and their friends found out, they criticized her for succumbing to peer pressure. They suggested that Nadja turn to the convent for advice. Returning from the convent, Nadja promptly went to school and returned her Comsomol card, saying that she did not need it anymore because she was leaving both that organization and the school. Neither persuasion nor threats by teachers helped. Nadja went to the police, returned her passport, and refused to take it back when they tried to force it on her. Still, they pushed the passport into her hands. Nadja tore it into pieces which she threw down on the table in front of the flabbergasted officials. Then Nadja went straight to the Tashkent convent. Her behavior was unheard of, and as a result, the police, collaborating with the Cheka, arrested the entire convent. The whole event was classified as a particularly serious crime against the state. Each nun received ten years.

In the Soviet Union, convent life differs little from life in camps, at least in terms of food, since the convents are so poor that the nuns must eat bread and "kasha," barley stew. The state does not support the convents. Their only subsidy is from the church to which the convent is attached, however the church, without a congregation, usually lacks funds. The income of many churches does not cover their expenses, let alone necessary repairs like fixing the roof or walls or replacing glass in the windows which are frequently broken by the local Comsomols.

The Tashkent convent was in a particularly bad situation because it did not belong to the official church and was considered illegal. The Orthodox church and its ministers are recognized by the state whereas the True Orthodox believers are considered a sect to be persecuted. The True Orthodox believers, on the other hand, believe that they alone possess the true faith. They sever themselves from the official leadership of the Orthodox churches which have, along with the priests, sold out to the Communist party, the Cheka, and the state censorship. The True Orthodox believers do not recognize these Orthodox ministers.

Prayer, the main occupation of the nuns, frequently lasted several hours. They kneeled for hours, reciting prayers and making signs of the cross. While dressing in the morning, they made the sign of the cross over each piece of clothing. Each piece of bread and each cup of water recieved its cross, as did the bed, in the evening before going to sleep. The nuns usually did not reveal their family names. If asked, they answered: "God's servant Barbara" or "God's servant Maria."

At the approach of Easter the nuns started their great fast, living on bread, water, and prayer for weeks on end. Their toughness was admirable. No inmates of the women's camps were more persecuted than the nuns. One would think the administration was trying to destroy the nuns. The hard punishment cells were probably not lifethreatening in summer, but we could not understand how the nuns endured these cement cubicles for weeks on end during the winter months, without heat or bedcovers. Warm food was issued once every two days, and the soup could be better described as dishwater. The other days they received only bread and water. It was bitter, bitter cold in the cubicles, and water froze.

When the thirty days of punishment passed, and the nuns came out of incarceration, all the women not stuck at their sew-

Orthodox nuns coming from punishment cell

ing machines ran up breathlessly to see how the nuns looked when they were carried out. Incredibly, the nuns walked out under their own power supporting each other. And yet it was a gloomy sight. Two of the younger nuns who could barely stand were propping up two elderly nuns, one of whom appeared ready to collapse. Not a drop of blood in her face, she looked like a wooden statue. The others did not look much better, except that they appeared to have a small residue of strength. The nuns took a long time to cross the small stretch between the punishment cells and the gate where the other nuns waited to take the emaciated old women in their arms.

141

Then two of them flanked each of the others. The nuns walked to the barracks in a more sprightly step. Watching this sight and knowing of their stay on the frosty cement for thirty days, I could only believe God gave them the spiritual and physical strength to keep from perishing.

CHAPTER 14

OLGA VSEVOLODOVNA

Two or three days after my arrival in the camp, Erna introduced me to Olga Vsevolodovna Ivinskaya, explaining that she was in the camp in connection with Boris Pasternak's book *Doctor Zhivago.* The newspapers carried abusive articles about Pasternak. But Olga Vsevolodovna was never mentioned in Latvian newspapers. She was Pasternak's secretary and mistress. I wanted to hear in her own words how she arrived here. It seemed illogical that Pasternak wrote a book which he gave to an Italian journalist. Then instead of jailing the writer, they arrested Olga Vsevolodovna after his death!

When I met her, I was surprised at how different Olga was from the other women prisoners. Though no longer young, and imprisoned for a number of years, she literally bloomed. She was the only one in the whole camp who did not look like a prisoner. Her skin was beautiful, pale and pure as Japanese porcelain. Her smile was like a warm caress. She radiated peace and kindness, and it felt good to be near her. Her beautiful blonde hair, naturally wavy was arranged in a loose knot at the nape in a hairstyle that could have competed with that of a high society lady at the beginning of the century. Her appearance and style were extraordinary under prison conditions.

In spite of her well groomed and pampered appearance, she proved to have immense moral strength. Olga was always kind, and never displayed bad temper. Unlike the other prisoners, she never appeared nervous. It was a special treat to listen when she spoke. No one in the camp spoke Russian as beautifully; besides, she possessed a fine literary style.

I told her briefly about myself. After hearing the accusations against me. Olga was astonished and reported that many people in Moscow kept the kind of literature for which I was convicted in their homes, but that no one was taken to court for it. Then I asked her: "I do not understand why you are here. As far as I know, Boris Pasternak gave his manuscript to the Italians himself."

"That's true, he gave it to them himself. But in his will he left all the Zhivago income to me. When Pasternak left us, I received parcels of the Zhivago money from abroad. That's what I was condemned for."

"With what right? For what?" I exclaimed.

"They have unlimited rights and powers, and if they want to pick on someone they always find a way. They condemned not only me, but my daughter also. We were accused of black market activity, and placed in camp #6 like common speculators, along with the most awful women criminals. These are all, in the language of the jurists, crimes against the collective."

"And then, what happened?"

"I wrote to the Ministry of the Interior, asking for permission to serve our time in this camp because the company in camp #6 was very unsuited to so young a girl as my daughter. One heard only curses and obscenities. I would never have believed that women of that kind exist in this world. In two weeks there we never heard a decent sentence. Even the songs they shrieked were filled with obscenities. After two weeks we received permission to serve our sentence in a camp for prisoners condemned for crimes against the state, and we were brought here. My daughter's sentence was only three years, she is at home already. I received five years."

"But, I don't understand, what did you have to do with the black market?"

"In the parcels from abroad there were clothes and things that neither of us could use. Since we had no money to pay our rent, we sold the things that we could not use."

144

"I still think the black market clause was applied to you incorrectly. It seems to me that you are involved in the black market if you buy something for the state price and sell it for a higher one, thus gaining a profit."

"Yes my dear, that's what you and many others think. But they wanted to get us into prison. We were an irritation."

"It would mean that, if my aunt gave me a piano which I sell because I don't play or have room for it, then within a week I could be arrested and tried as a speculator!" I blurted out indignantly.

"That's the way it is. We are powerless to change it."

After this first conversation I thought about her situation and smoldered again at the Soviet institutions of power. I recalled the Russian proverb: "All we need is the man, the law against him can always be found."

Olga Vsevolodovna's health was poor, but she was not assigned to the invalid group. She worked in the sewing shop where she trimmed the thread ends of the finished products with scissors because she could not learn to use the machines.

Once the two of us were sitting on a small bench outside the barrack. There was no one else about, so she recited a few excerpts from *Dr. Zhivago* for me. Most people remain ignorant of the controversial works of literature if the newspapers do not print slanderous articles. After reading these attacks, people try to read the literary work. However most remain in ignorance about the actual content of the novel, story, or poem so abused in the press.

When Olga finished her recitation, she smiled, but then warned me in hushed voice: "If I were you, I would watch myself a little with the reptile."

"With the reptile?" I asked in confusion. "What do you mean?"

"Your friend Erna. She reminds me of a reptile, and that's what I have been calling her from the first day I saw her."

"Thank you," was all that I could say, for I had to consider what she meant. A year passed before I discovered that Olga Vsevolodovna's remark was well founded. Generally, she trusted people, even too much so, but in this case she had not been mistaken in calling Erna "Reptilia," as I learned later.

Olga remained fit for years, however in her last years in the camp she ailed more and more often. She walked slowly and sometimes she was not able to rise from her bed. No medicine helped, and it was painful to watch her becoming paler and thinner. She had a good friend among the nuns who brought her food and helped her when she could not get up. When she felt ill, I did not want to impose lengthy conversations on her, and we only exchanged a few words. Even then, though I could see she was in pain, she usually had a friendly smile. Warmth dominated her personality. Her cordiality was artless, pure as the sunshine itself. With it, she gained the friendship and respect of others.

No matter how slowly time passed in the camp, the day came when Olga Vsevolodovna said good-bye. Tears in her eyes, she embraced each of us in turn. She wished from the bottom of her heart that the rest of us were coming home with her. She told some of us her address, inviting us to visit her in Moscow.

We were glad for every one who departed, though we knew the difficulties of entering "freedom" after imprisonment.

CHAPTER 15

NATALIA

After the ordeal of interrogations and courts, some new prisoners felt relief and adjusted easily to camp life.

While the difficulties, humiliations and starvation of camp life are not yet known, the camp appears to newcomers like a mirage in the desert. This mirage is especially true in summer. With flowers blooming all around and birds singing in the trees, the camp appears as a welcome change after the jails and boxcars. Such was not the case with one new prisoner.

On a sunny, summer day, a new arrival came into the zone, sat down on the bench nearest the gate and began to cry. A well–dressed, gray-haired stout lady, she almost filled the whole bench. She cried through dinner. She refused supper too, and only after the evening roll call was she willing to come to bed. Without a word she lay down and continued to cry. If she had not breathed a few "no, thank you's," "it's nothing," "thank you," we would have thought her to be a deaf-mute. Not until the next day did she tell us briefly what happened. And what happened was so extraordinary that it aroused the whole camp.

She introduced herself, "My name is Natalia Franzovna." This form of introduction, by name and patronymic, indicated that she expected to be respected, and was used to such treatment. Natalia's language, manner, and movements were correct and refined. In spite of her size, she moved gracefully.

She started to speak, "Women," she began in a soft voice, "none of you can imagine the cruel fate I have met." She paused and continued. "In 1948 I was given twenty-five years. In 1956, when everyone was released after the great commission, I too was released. I organized my life, worked, raised my daughter who had lived in an orphanage for eight years. And suddenly, after seven years, I am brought here and told that I have to serve the remaining seventeen years."

There was an uneasy silence, then a voice stated, "It is obvious the era of Stalin has returned."

After wiping her tears, which streamed over her cheeks, she continued, "I asked why I was arrested. And without blinking an eye, he said, 'According to the will of the nation. I can explain nothing more. If there is something you do not like, when you are at the camp, write whomever you want to. I have orders to get you to the camp. Tomorrow you will go on transport!' With that the conversation was ended and I, in a state of utter confusion, was taken to the cell."

"But your belongings, underwear, clothes . . . how did you get those?" someone asked.

"After my insistent pleas the head of the prison allowed two armed soldiers to take me to my house to fetch clothes. Obviously, they had no clothes my size in the prison storerooms, and so they had no choice."

She spoke no more, as she started to cry again. Everyone understood that her case was extraordinary and that she suffered severely. For several days there was great unrest in the camp and many felt that those released after the great commission in 1956 would return again. Natalia was a living example. No one was indifferent to her case, which involved seventeen years. Everyone knew that the highest penalty was fifteen years. Those with a twenty-five year sentence feared they would have to serve the whole sentence instead of the fifteen-year maximum introduced by the new law. The worry affected the health of several inmates, resulting in heart attacks, insomnia, and other nervous ailments.

When Natalia calmed down, she began to write complaints and requests about her case to Moscow. She did not mind reading them to the others, she had no secrets. Her case was exactly as she explained. The only thing we could not understand was what "nation" wanted Natalia to return to prison. What kind of nation was it and where was it located? What was Natalia's relationship with the nation? In 1956 Natalia settled in a city in Siberia, far from her former residence. No one knew her. She worked in the drug store, was kind to people, and was easy to get along with. What kind of nation was it? Natalia revealed her secret. Regardless of the circumstances in which women live, the curious ones are usually also talkative. "The nation" demanding that Natalia spend another seventeen years in prison was her husband. Natalia made no secret of it. She was highly indignant that the Cheka could call one man a nation.

Meanwhile, an article appeared in one of the Moscow newspapers saying that Natalia Franzovna Greenwald deliberately chose to live in a remote place to evade her penalty. The nation's alert eye had spotted her and rendered her harmless, so that she would not escape serving the just sentence for her terrible crime. The "nation" was the signatures of three men, whom Natalia did not know. The camp director brought in the newspaper which went from hand to hand. Natalia was indignant about the article and the fact that the Cheka used complete strangers against her.

Natalia received the news that her husband, fifteen years younger and now rid of his wife, was selling their belongings, actually bought by her. Before the law their property belonged equally to husband and wife. Even though in Siberia, their city apartment was well furnished with rugs, a television, and a refrigerator. As he was selling the property, the husband obviously intended to move; money is always easier to transport than furniture. However, to throw a wife of seven years into prison is not the testimony to a good man.

Natalia received answers from Moscow that what happened was lawful and correct. According to the new law, she must serve not twenty-five but fifteen years, of which the eight previously served were credited to her. Seven remained. Natalia, of course, was not satisifed. She redoubled her writing efforts to gain a court trial to which as a citizen of the U.S.S.R., she had full right.

In 1948, when she was first arrested, there was no court procedure. She was brought into prison one day, then called into a room before three uniformed men. There was no investigation, prosecutor, judge, or lawyer. The men simply announced that she, Natalia Franzovna Greenwald, received twenty-five years imprisonment to be spent in the corrective labor camp. Her sentence was final, without right of appeal. This three-man court without investigation was common at the time. This kind of trial was fast, and required no records or personnel. It made no difference anyway, because then everyone received twenty-five years, with or without an investigation.

Natalia wanted a regular court trial with papers, witnesses, investigation, and court procedure, with prosecutor and lawyer present. She wanted to be tried according to current laws, not by those of a system long out of existence. Her demands were justified. But her complaints achieved no results because no one wanted to accept the responsibility to review her case. If nothing could be proved against her, Natalia would have to be acquited. So great a penalty could not be changed when eight years had already been served and she was again imprisoned. This would mean that the Cheka's right hand did not know what the left hand was doing. Since such a disgrace could not be hushed up, it was better to leave things as they were.

Natalia calmed down, and finding herself in congenial company, related more about her life. That war, how much misfortune it has brought humanity! I had a good husband, a daughter, and we were living a normal life, until the war started and destroyed everything. The Germans shot and killed my husband. I was taken to Czechoslovakia to work in a factory. My child stayed with my parents, who were still alive and had their own little house."

"And how did you return after the war?" asked Nina, who seated herself a little closer.

"In Czechoslovakia many women workers from Russia were placed in boxcars and brought back."

"Was there any attempt to imprison you then?"

"Not the women, only the men. I came home, stayed with my parents, my daughter started school, and I got a job in a drug store. Then after one month I was suddenly taken directly to prison. There I was told the Germans shot my husband because I betrayed him. I was too startled to speak. My words would have made no difference."

"But that is wrong. How can the accusation come without any witnesses?"

"There was not a single witness to say one word for or against me," Natalia explained and fell silent.

150

"And you ended up in the camp?" It was obvious that the questioner did not want the conversation to end.

"Yes, at that time the camps were large; our camp contained a couple of thousand. There was a shortage of people with medical training. There was a lot of work giving minimal aid to the sick women. I worked in the medical office. Often the patients made their own diagnosis, pointing with their hands to the part that hurt. In the camp there was no special medication, only pain killers, heart drops, and medicine for stomach aches."

"How primitive!"

"Any reasonably knowledgeable woman could manage the ten medicine labels and the thermometer. But serious cases did come up which required a doctor. Sometimes it was even possible to save the patient, if she was taken to the hospital in time, and if the doctor's diagnosis was correct: an inflamed appendix rather than cirrhosis of the liver."

"I thought the doctors came from among prisoners at that time."

"That is true. But it is not always possible to diagnosis correctly without special equipment. At that time the camp medical level was medieval. It seems to be no better now," Natalia added venomously, nodding towards the medical office.

"Were there a lot of deaths in the women's camp?"

"In general, yes, but not nearly as many as in the men's camps. Men were dying as fast as if death were stalking through the camps, mowing grass. The women did the same work in the woods on the same food in the same circumstances, but showed much greater endurance."

"How?"

"One possibility is that men are by nature not as frugal. In the morning, when the day's bread ration was handed out, most of the men consumed it immediately. They saved nothing for the evening. Then the whole day until the next morning was spent without bread, which had a bad effect on the digestive system. The women, on the other hand, carried their bread ration with them and broke off small pieces several times during the day. This way they were never satisfied, but neither did they starve for long periods."

"And what was it like in 1955, when the great commission was announced?"

"Those were unforgettable days. To begin with, we found it hard to believe the news. But when the commission actually arrived, people cried with joy. Every day several dozen went home."

"But not everyone was released. This camp contains a number of people who did not get out, and the men's camp has many more."

"I am still here from those times," said a middle-aged woman from the Ukraine.

"Yes, I discovered that here. But while I was still in the camp, everyone was released. When I was called before the commission, my sentence was read in five minutes. It was announced that the commission, upon reviewing my case, decided that I spent enough time in prison and was dropping the rest of my sentence. The next day I left the punitive zone to return home. It was the same for everyone."

"Was there any order or system by which the release was carried out? Was the length of the sentence considered, or perhaps those with shorter sentences were released first?"

"The first ones released were the seriously ill and those whose sentences were nearly up. And then at random, without any particular method. When we came out through the gate, we felt confused and could not believe we were free. I sat with my two suitcases and did not know which way to turn. Then a young fellow, also released, talked to me. He had nothing to carry and offered to help carry my suitcases to the railway station. The suitcases were heavy, containing many handicrafts, gifts from the women whom I had helped with medication."

"He must have been a rare bird, to offer help. Was he a Russian?" Natalia's story was interrupted by Nina.

"Yes, he was a Russian. It's not possible to identify every scoundrel immediately. Some can pretend for years."

"Why a scoundrel? Did he steal your suitcases?" Nina's interest increased by the minute.

"Quite the opposite. He told me all sorts of good things about himself, promised to help me in every way, until I was willing to go with him, and we got married."

"What, on the spot?"

"Not quite, but almost. He exploited my confusion and my upset state. I cannot describe the great tension after sudden release. No one, who has not experienced it, can understand it. I wanted to cry and laugh at the same time. It was impossible to think. Few knew what they were doing. Most of us didn't even have a place to go. It is impossible to decide immediately. We knew that even with an early release, no one was waiting for us, or needed us. No one likes to know or befriend ex-prisoners. Even relatives sometimes will not receive us. So, it was not surprising that I was ready and willing to follow a complete stranger, as I had no relatives left, except my

daughter in an orphanage. Also, he was young and
strong, promised to work, so that we would be well off,
as he, too, was without family. At first we couldn't decide
where to go. I longed for familiar cities, like Moscow or
Leningrad. He convinced me that we couldn't go where
there would be no chance of finding an apartment and
getting registered."

"Well he was right."

"Exactly. He persuaded me so that I depended on him
and believed every word he said. He suggested Siberia,
where it would be possible to better ourselves fast and to
live well. At the industrial centers of Siberia workers
were always in demand and getting an apartment was
no problem. He explained this so logically that I was so
glad to have met him, thinking that fate had brought him
to me."

"You received an evil fate instead of good."

"It amounts to that. However in the beginning I
couldn't imagine it would end that way. We settled
nicely. We lived first in a rented room, then in an
apartment much nicer than any I could have imagined.
Then I brought my daughter. I worked in the drug store,
my husband in the factory. It seemed that nothing could
cast a shadow in our life."

Here she sighed, shed a few tears, and continued, "My parents died while I was in the camp, but an aunt was still alive. I
knew her address and once I had a permanent address, I wrote
to her. Much to my surprise she wrote that she wanted to give
me our family's valuables and money. My parents once were
quite well off. I received all that my parents left, except the furniture and clothes, which I gave to my kind aunt. Upon my
return, I immediately bought all that money can buy to make
life more pleasant: a T.V., carpets, a refrigerator, good furniture.
No one ever knows how long money will be valid. If a mone-
tary reform comes, all could be lost. And as soon as I spent the
money, a reform occurred and the money and prices changed.

With the new money, there was never enough. But now listen to what my husband was up to. While I was trying to improve our place and our life, he left work.

"At first he went off in the morning, as if he were going to work, and I knew nothing. I found out only after this was going on for six months, and he was not ashamed to stay home and sleep. When I asked why he didn't get up, he replied indifferently that he did not have to go to work. Money was often missing from the drawer. He informed me cynically that he borrowed it for card games. When I hid the money, valuables disappeared, which he borrowed to pawn or sell. Who could watch him when I had to be at work every day?"

"Was he a laborer?" Nina asked.

"He was a laborer, yes. He did not speak of his parents, but he was obviously from that background. Why do you ask?"

"The thought occurred to me that the Russian laborer is a good laborer as long as he wants to eat. As soon as he is satisfied, he does not want to work. It is the opposite with the intelligent Russian. As long as he has nothing, he drinks up his property. But as soon as an opportunity arises to break out of poverty, he works like crazy."

"Your comparison hit the nail on the head."

After a while, Nina asked, "Why didn't you get rid of the parasite?"

"I threatened him several times with the militia. Of course, I would never have done it, but what doesn't a person say when his heart if full? Secondly, because the apartment was in my husband's name, my daughter and I would have to leave, but everything in the apartment was bought with my money. How could I walk out into the street empty-handed? Often in my sorrow I wondered but was unable to find a solution. Until once during a sharp exchange he told me that my days were numbered if I continued to interfere in his life; I should be quiet and consider myself fortunate that he kept me under his roof. At the time I did not take these words seriously, and I could not imagine what he would do."

"I would feel very scared living with a person who told me my days were numbered," Nina commented.

"I thought things are said often in anger that are not really meant. But now, knowing the identity of the 'nation's will' everything became much clearer; obviously the rest of the 'nation' was his card-partners."

"You do not know them?"

"No, how could I? They did not come to our place and I considered it beneath my dignity to follow my husband to find out where he roamed."

"You should have explained to the Cheka that the 'nation' was your husband with whom you were at odds."

"The Cheka knew that, but I did not know it then."

"In that case the only solution to your case is the court."

"That's exactly what I am waiting for. Let's hope that someone will listen to me and give me the opportunity to appear in court."

Days went by, months, years, but no court for Natalia Franzovna. To all her requests and appeals regularly came the answer that she received the correct sentence and that a new investigation or court procedure would not be useful. After every answer Natalia cried for days, not knowing to whom to write next. No one had any advice to offer since her case was unique. From the tension and the frequent crying, Natalia lost weight. In the span of one year she shrank to one third her original size.

Once Natalia received some important guests who called themselves journalists from Kiev. For several hours they questioned her about her charges, about her relationship with her first husband, shot by the Germans. After several hours, they left. Natalia walked around in thought, at times in tears. Natalia knew the strange visitors were not interested in helping her, but only in satisfying their curiosity. They would not promise to help her, when she asked them.

In a few months the purpose of their visit became clear. A long article appeared in the newspaper, stating that Natalia Franzovna Greenwald was one of the greatest criminals of the century and that her crime provided the basis for a film being produced in Kiev. The article mentioned that Natalia served eight years previously, but was returned to the punitive camp by the will of the nation to serve her sentence in full. At length the article described the conscientiousness of the nation in helping the security forces to detect and unmask such a dangerous state criminal. The people who requested that Natalia be returned to the punitive camp were considered ideological leaders.

The newspaper passed from hand to hand. Every woman wanted to read the article with her own eyes. As Natalia told us, she was accused of betraying her husband, who was active in the Kiev underground, to the Gestapo. Several others from the underground were shot by the Gestapo. Natalia was accused of betraying four people, receiving as payment clothes taken from the dead people. Knowing Natalia, the story about the clothes sounded unbelievable. It was difficult to imagine her putting on something another had worn. Besides, she could earn money through her profession.

After the appearance of the article, opinion divided among the women in the camp. The majority thought that Natalia fell into disfavor and that the article was not true. It is well known that in cases where the jurists of the Cheka knew their accusations were unfounded and could not be proved, they used the newspaper to persuade people to believe their lies about the guilt of the accused. However other women thought maybe she was guilty. When one of the inmates asked Natalia how the Gestapo had detected her husband and his friends, she said through a betrayal.

"I strongly suspected an actress who was known to participate in concerts for the higher German officers. The same actress knew the underground men."

After the appearance of the article, Natalia cried every day. Everyone understood that nothing would change her case. Hope now vanished that a court trial could convince the judges and prosecutors of her innocence. It was painful to watch this gray-haired lady for whom nothing remained but tears. During the time she sent letters to the All–Soviet Prosecutor's Office and the Ministry of Justice, she did not cry. Now however she had nothing to do. In the span of a few weeks, she withered dramatically.

Natalia clearly recognized her destiny, one shared by many other women. According to the Soviet law, only those with at least twenty-five years of service have a right to an old-age pension. The years spent in prisons and camps do not count, even though the inmates have to work forty-eight hours a week. If an elderly woman is released after spending twenty-five years in the correction camp, she has to work for another twenty-five years in order to receive a pension from the state. If her health has been destroyed in prison and she is unable to work, she has no choice but the poorhouse.

From camp #17-A several women went straight to the poorhouse under escort, after they finished their sentence. There the circumstances are slightly better than in prison. At the camp many women had no other prospects. Now Natalia Franzovna joined their ranks, because at the time of her release she would be seventy years old with destroyed health.

CHAPTER 16

LYDIA

A few weeks passed since my arrival in camp #17-A. I became acquainted with almost all of the women, except Lydia. Concerned with her own affairs, she did not care who entered or left the camp. She was so busy that often she did not come to the dining room to eat. Though Lydia often went without lunch or dinner, neither her looks suffered, nor did she lose weight; on the contrary, she blossomed like a rose. Lydia worked as the designer and main cutter in the sewing shop. This was her specialty, even on the outside.

What Lydia cut and designed none of us ever saw. We saw that she got along well with the administration and that all sorts of people came and went from the place. She had a separate room where she worked from early morning till late night. Sometimes Lydia even smelled of wine. She was always by herself, never making friends with any of the prisoners.

Although already imprisoned for ten years, she looked as though she had served ten days at the most. Five years remained. It was evident that Lydia was not serving a political sentence because people interested in or occupied with political activity need connections with, and information from, fellow prisoners. Lydia studiously avoided contact with others.

One day I asked Nina: "Say, do you know anything about Lydia? You know everyone. Lydia never speaks about herself."

"She doesn't need to; anyone who wants to find out about her, can."

"What do you mean?"

"On the outside, did you see the movie *Quiet Journey?*"

"No, what is it about?"

Lydia

"It's about Lydia and her lover."

"What? A movie about Lydia?"

"Yes, some magazine carried an account of her crime. Later apparently they made a movie of it. The magazine was passed from hand to hand here in the camp. They promised to show the film to us, but it never got here."

"Then Lydia is a famous personality. But what actually happened?"

"Lydia and her lover planned to escape abroad. They plotted to use a plane because her lover was a pilot. When they were in the plane, ready to take off, something went wrong, and they resorted to the final solution, murder. He killed two pilots, but the third one, though seriously injured, remained alive."

"Why did Lydia get such a heavy sentence?"

"She got fifteen years for handing him the knife to kill the pilots."

"And the man?"

"Him? Of course he got the maximum, death."

"Maybe that's why Lydia doesn't talk to anyone, because of her suffering. I assume his sentence was executed."

"Lydia suffering! What do you take her for? She suffering for somebody? Money is her god, she cares nothing about people. Why do you think she sits in the workshop from early morning to late evening? Because it is in her interest."

"But, if she is an accomplice in murder with no political involvement, why is she in our camp?"

"It's considered political because she wanted to escape abroad."

"Do you think everybody who wants to go abroad has political reasons?"

"Not everyone does, of course. I imagine the great majority have a purely materialistic reason. In spite of her long sentence and serious charge, she has made herself at home here. She lacks nothing, she lives like a bug in a rug."

"Aren't outsiders afraid to deal with a prisoner? They risk a sentence of up to two years if they are caught."

"They trust Lydia, knowing that she would not betray anyone. These are good contacts established long ago. That's why she does not talk or become friendly with anybody here."

Helene Celmina

"Now I understand. It would be against her interests to lose her good relationship with the outsiders by talking with prisoners."

"Since she is on such good terms with the administration, does she get packages from home?"

"She could if there was someone to send them to her."

"Doesn't she have relatives?"

"A daughter."

"But if she has been here for ten years, the girl must have been quite small."

"She was about seven or eight years old, her grandmother was still alive. When the grandmother died, Lydia wrote the neighbors not to let the orphanage take the little girl. They were kind, sympathetic neighbors and kept the girl."

"That's rare that somebody would take in a strange child. It's also expensive."

"Lydia sent money for the child's expenses."

"What? Sending things from a camp to the outside? Can that be done? How could she make money here?"

"Several mothers here send money to their children. You can do it by submitting a written request to the supervisor, asking that an amount be deducted from your personal money and sent to the address on the request. Naturally most earn so little that they cannot send more than ten rubles a month to their children. The great majority recieve nothing for their labor and can send nothing. The only ones who earn anything are those who have been working in the sewing shop for years. Lydia is an exception. She earns the most and can send

162

the most. I heard she sends no less than thirty rubles to her daughter every month."

A few months later, Lydia spoke to me. Briefly and matter of factly she explained that her eighteen year old daughter was to be married soon. She wanted me to paint a sizeable oil painting as a wedding gift. She would send one thousand rubles for her wedding, but she would also like to send a gift.

"But will they let you send the painting out of the camp?"

"Don't worry, I already spoke with the administration. In a case like this, they let you."

"What about the canvas?"

"I will get you canvas. I will give you more canvas than you need so there is some left for you. Make the painting as large as you can. I think we can agree on payment. It seems to me you smoke. How about cigarettes?"

I felt dizzy for joy that she was offering cigarettes and accepted before she could change her mind.

A few days later Lydia gave me a nice length of canvas. We agreed on the size of the painting, the subject was still left open. I mentioned that, if she could sit for me, I could paint her portrait. At first Lydia considered this but then energetically said, "No, that would not do. My son-in-law might not like to have on his wall a mother-in-law who is in prison. A landscape would be better."

I brought a whole pile of picture postcards, Latvian landscapes, sent to me in the mail. She chose one, and I went to work.

Lydia paid me with cigarettes, and even threw in a handful of candy. I did not ask where these goodies came from because the camp store never had these.

One could survive in the camp where there is no equality, though reading the internal rules plastered on the walls suggest that the camp was the only place where complete and uncompromising equality reigned.

CHAPTER 17

CLARA

The arrival of a transport was a major event in the life of camp #17-A because often a whole month passed during which nothing happened. For months on end, the names, surnames, and numbers of the imprisoned women remained the same in the camp rosters. It was a rare occurence when the term of a prisoner ended; a pardon was even rarer. A shipment of new prisoners was quite uncommon. If anyone was brought in, she was usually alone. This time, however, eleven arrived.

Around noon the gates opened, and all the prisoners in the yard glanced up curiously. A nun in black garb appeared, then another one behind her, a teenager, her face barely visible behind a white kerchief. More black-garbed nuns followed, one after the other. All the newcomers took five or six steps, set down small bundles containing their personal belongings and stood together silently. All wore long skirts and the regulation capelike headdress hanging over the shoulders. At a distance, their black figures formed one compact mass. The white-kerchiefed teenager stood off by herself.

Usually, upon the arrival of a new inmate, everyone rushed forward to get acquainted. This time, nobody rushed to meet the new arrivals because we knew that the nuns were not sociable, and probably did not wish to talk. One woman went inside the barracks to tell the nuns in the camp that others had arrived. Immediately, several ran out and rushed across the yard to the newcomers. The fluttering black cloaks presented a strange sight. Because of their black robes and sedate movements, the nuns seemed old. Now however, one would have thought they had been promised a gold medal in a race. Judging from the greetings at the gate, these nuns evidently were old acquaintances reunited, after long separation.

One after another, the slower nuns gathered around, forming a large black crowd. Everyone wanted to get close to the new ones, to embrace each of them in turn and to kiss them again and again. Only the teenager remained separate.

While I watched uncomprehending, Valentina Semjonovna joined me. She looked at the black group and then said, "They did come after all."

"Who came?" I asked.

"Well the nuns, don't you see?"

"I see they are nuns and they seem to be acquainted with our nuns."

"They are all from our camp."

"Where were they then?"

"Why they were in the Vladimir Prison of course! Didn't you know that some of our people are always in Vladimir?"

"I didn't realize that there were so many. I thought two, three at the most."

"There are always several nuns and a few others. Tatjana also sat in Vladimir for three years."

Valya came out of the building onto the porch, lit a cigarette, and after watching the doings at the gate, also hurried over. She approached the teenager. They embraced and came towards me, engaged in friendly conversation. When they both passed me, I saw that the teenager was no less than forty years old. It is always difficult to tell the age of women who have long been imprisoned.

Because of her slight build, light hair, and blue eyes, she appeared to be a teenager with an old face. Her blue eyes were innocent as a child's, but her tightly closed lips, with the lines deeply graven in the corners told of long suffering. Her yellow, mummified face testified to many years of imprisonment. In the bright afternoon sun, her skin resembled yellow parchment carefully stretched over the skull. But for her prominent blue

Clara

eyes, she looked dead. Her name was unusual like herself: Clara Kleiman. She wasn't Russian.

Looking at Clara, I was reminded of an old clock that has never been wound. Such a clock could be called both old and new. Clara's appearance suggested experience and self assurance. She was not one to establish contacts quickly or let herself be drawn into conversations with strangers. Clara never talked without need. In the living section of the barracks, she approached the bed in which she apparently had slept for several months and asked dryly, "Who is sleeping in this bed?" Clara sought the woman out and announced, in a voice that would entertain no objection, that she wished to occupy her old bed. The other woman, one of the religious prisoners who never resisted the desires of others, naturally acquiesced.

Then the superintendent of the camp told the woman about to take her bedclothes, "You stay where you are. Kleiman has to take the bed over there." She pointed to an empty bed in the middle of the room.

Clara gave the superintendent a contemptuous look and announced, "You can have that bed, Citizen Jailer."

The supervisor's face flushed a deep and angry red at such impudence. Barely controlling herself, yet in a pointedly polite tone she answered, "Prisoner Kleiman, you forget where you are. Perhaps I should remind you."

Clara, just as politely responded, "No, Citizen Jailer, I do not need your reminder, and if you don't like my looks, you can send me back to Vladimir. At least I have peace there."

"We will see about that," replied the other, still aflame with anger.

Clara remained livid. "Just imagine, trying to tell me in which bed I should sleep! She can do that to someone who comes to visit the prison for a year or two, but not to someone who's spent half of her life here. This woman, who can't even wipe her own nose, has the nerve to touch me! I'd like to see her in a coffin wearing white slippers, this all-knowing supervisor. I need her like a hole in the head. She should go and wash her own feet instead." Clara had a point, the supervisor did have dirty feet.

While this incident occurred, the other woman stripped the bed and Clara started making herself at home. As Clara's bed was directly opposite mine I watched her get settled. Somewhere, she garnered her own sheets, which she fastened to the lower edge of the upper bunk, strung on a line like curtains. Clara was ready to "live" in her bed. She had no intention of going to work. She sat in her bed for days on end. She embroidered with great patience and care. Her work was detailed, complicated, and so well executed that it appeared to be machine work. Once she pulled several finished pieces from her pillow to show me. I praised her work, but wondered where she got so many new sheets to cut up. The prison shop does not sell muslin, and there was no way to send her any from home to Vladimir Prison.

She was sent to Vladimir for the same offense as the nuns: refusing to work. On the days when Clara did not do needlework, she read books borrowed from the others. Often she read magazines, *Science and Technology* or *Around the World*. I did not ask why she was in prison because she was a moody person, and would not answer questions if she was in a bad mood. From time to time Clara would get into a bad temper, climb into bed, and pull her sheet curtain shut. Nobody dared disturb her. She lay in her bed for days at a time. She came to the dining hall for meals, but returned to bed immediately.

The supervisor did not bother Clara, apparently feeling that she would only cause trouble for herself and the rest of the camp administration. Clara was left alone. Even though she refused to work, they did not put her in a punishment cell.

A woman once asked Clara why she did not go to work, "After all," she said, "it shortens the time, and one does not have to fear the cell."

Clara listened quitly and answered, "I am here to serve my sentence, not to increase the property of the state."

That was well said, but not everyone has the will to hold out for years against the rule. Much depends on one's personality. Most people need something to do during imprisonment. Some women have said publicly that they could not endure without work, and that they would probably kill themselves if the prisons took it away. Even Clara doesn't sit idly, as her fine stitching showed.

Days, weeks, and months passed, until one day important guests from Moscow arrived in camp #17-A. The local administrators explained that they were a commission from Moscow. The overseers ran around making sure there was no litter and that our zone was in order. Then they ran into the living section to make sure that the beds were nicely made and uncluttered. Seeing a cat curled up on one of the beds, an overseer grabbed a towel and swung at the cat which, in panic, ran for the window. On the windowsill was a pot with a bright red fuchsia blooming in it. Another overseer ran to open the door for the cat. It was too late. The pot lay in shards and the floor was strewn with dirt. Of course the few old women who happened to be near were told to clean it up.

First the visitors went to the work zone, then to the living section. Usually they stopped by the door, never entering the room. They looked, and passed on. This time would have been no different if Clara had not been present. She was, as usual, squatting in her nest. When the commission arrived, she came out on the porch. Seeing such a large group of officers in uniforms, Clara approached slowly as though taking a leisurely walk. When she reached the officers her slender figure appeared to shrink, since the men were tall and stout. Clara stopped in the middle of their path and smiled innocently in a friendly fashion. The inevitable happened, one of the unsuspecting officers glanced at her and asked how she was. Waiting for this opportunity she spoke so fluently that an observer might have thought that she memorized and rehearsed her speech. When one speaks the truth however, one does not need preparation; The truth comes out and wants to be heard by the ears of unbelievers.

Clara described in detail the conditions of the camp. She explained how we were robbed by the male criminals who cooked the meals, threw cigarette butts into the food, often spit, and even urinated into the soup. Once a piece of bicycle tire was found in the soup. She complained that the bread was heavy, bitterly sour, and soggy compared to that in other camps. Clara explained that these disgraces were reported to our administration, which smiled, did nothing, and intended to do nothing. She asked who was in charge of food and insisted that these disgraces be eliminated. Clara recited these grievances in a loud voice so that everyone could hear.

Listening with obvious distaste, the visitors could do little since Clara stood in their way. Nobody could interrupt Clara's flow of words, but as soon as she stopped to draw a breath, the supervisor hastened to explain and assure everyone that Clara was exaggerating. Again this opportunity was what Clara was waiting for. A tornado followed as she poured forth years of bitterness. Words rushed over her lips like water tumbling over the dam. Long experience taught her what to say, and she defended the minimal rights of these imprisoned women with knowledge and skill. In reference to the food problem, Clara recited verbatum the rations legislated for each person per day. She also explained to the commission why the camp administration permitted the male criminals of the neighboring zone to steal from the women of camp #17-A. Eighty percent of the prisoners in camp #17-A were condemned for religious activity. Knowing that these women would never lodge any complaints anywhere, the administration shamelessly exploited the situation, to exorcise their faith in God through hunger. Clara stressed that the administration hated religious prisoners and employed the most inhuman methods against them.

The rest, the non-religious prisoners, amounted to only twenty percent, half of whom were old women who would never complain about the local administration, especially since many of them did not know how to write. If any of the others tried to complain about the conditions, they received no response. If they had been political prisoners, Clara emphasized, the camp administration would have been compelled to accede to their demands according to written law.

Clara was right; each word was a strong accusation. Beyond fear, she defended strongly the prisoner's rights. Several times, she stressed that the times had passed when the prisoner had no rights and could be dealt with as the administration chose. If anyone doubted her words, he could look at the wall in the section where the rules of the prisons and camps were framed under glass. "There," Clara pointed in the direction of our barracks, "it is all there, black on white, in clear Russian—what we may do, and what we may not, what are your rights, and what are ours."

The visitors edged toward the exit. Clara pursued them, never letting the distance between herself and the guests diminish. She saw them to the gate, accusing them uninterruptedly of being the greatest violators of the law, of imprisoning innocent people who had never harmed anyone, and who were serving time because of their faith or their convictions. At last the visitors reached the gate, and one after another disappeared into the guard house. Even when they were outside the fence, Clara continued to speak. As they disappeared she added that they ought to be imprisoned. The women praised Clara for her true and accurate remarks. Suddenly, Clara exploded at them, "And you, you all stood there as though the cat got your tongues. When the administration can't hear, you moan and groan, but when you should speak, you clam up. What am I, a salaried defender?"

Now their mouths were shut, too. They wanted no quarrel with Clara. After the excitement of her speech, Clara's mood improved. I admired this tiny woman whose pointed and exact complaints forced a whole crowd of officers to retreat. She literally drove them out of the zone. Her last words at the gate were, "You have no business here if you don't want to or cannot improve our conditions."

This incident confirmed my earlier supposition that Clara

had a lot of experience. A few days later, I expressed my admiration for her judgment of the illegalities in the camp. Clara remarked that this was not her first encounter and that the prison laws were as familiar to her as the A-B-Cs. Clara had already served twenty-three years of a twenty-five year sentence. Thirty-nine now, she was arrested at fifteen-and-a-half. Though her mother and daughter, who was born in prison, lived outside in Yalta, no one had written to Clara in twenty-two years.

"Because my mother is a doctor and wanted to continue working as one, she was forced to renounce me. From then on, we have had no contact. I am grateful to her for taking my little girl because otherwise she would have gone to the orphanage, and we all know what grows up there."

"What you are saying is tragic. In the past they have forced people to renounce undesirable family members, but relatives are no longer persecuted for transgressions of their kin. I think you would have difficulty finding a family in which someone has not been imprisoned. It is so common that people speak about it openly."

"What you say is true, but my mother does not write to me." A human being can get used to anything. Do you want to hear something really terrible?" Clara grinned conspiringly. "When I was twenty I was in Kalima. Men and women worked together cutting timber in the woods. Three men prepared to escape and promised to take me along if I wanted to join them. Of course, I said yes. We hoarded as much dried bread as we could hide under our clothing. A shortage of bread in the camps at that time made it difficult to save up a small supply to take along. On the appointed day we escaped. At first we walked day and night, through taiga. On the fourth day our food was gone. We went two days without eating, hoping to find something, but there was nothing in the taiga. Finally we decided we had no choice but to draw lots with matches to see who would be eaten. The match pointed at me. We were silent, then the organizer of the escape stood up and announced, 'We are real men, and we will not eat our only woman. We are going back to camp, there is no other way.' Because it was the law to obey the eldest, we returned to camp. It took us ten days to cover the same ground that previously took six. The return journey was so horrible, it cannot be described. There were no roads, and

weakened as we were, our feet kept getting caught on clumps
of grass. We were at the end of our strength when we reached
camp, stumbling, bruised and scratched."

The "who's going to eat whom" part of Clara's story gave
me a cold shiver, and I wondered what kind of people could
say such words. Later I heard from Clara and others of numerous cases where two escapees took a third along, as a "cow,"
previously marked for food, of course without his knowledge.

Clara continued, "We didn't get much punishment because
we returned voluntarily. Even the hardest heart felt pity at the
sight of us. Each received sixty days and sixty nights of solitary.
The cell would have been restful if the approach of winter had
not made the unheated cells cold at night. My only salvation
was my hair. I loosened my long braids and wrapped myself in
my hair and felt halfway warm. My legs and feet were cold but
I thought of the poor men who had no long hair at all."

After Clara's tale, I could not sleep. I still didn't know why
she was in prison. Because her story about Kalima could only
refer to the criminal prisoners, she appeared to be a criminal
prisoner later condemned for a political offense. No matter who
or what she was, I felt a certain respect for her.

The regard that the others felt for Clara was due to her independent attitude toward the camp administration. She hadn't
lost her feisty attitude through her many years of imprisonment. This was especially striking because criminal prisoners
usually came to accept the prison administration, in order to
gain its good will and material compensation, tea. The criminal
prisoners literally idolize tea, for which they are willing to
carry out all the administration's orders and even work all
night. Tea was more valuable to them than cigarettes. From this
tea, they make a narcotic drink, Chifir, brewing forty grams of
black tea to each half liter of water.

Though our beds were opposite each other, several weeks
passed before I had a chance to speak to Clara. She was in no
mood for conversation. Like a little girl, she played with the cat
which she trained to sleep in her bed. Flattered by the attention,
the cat gladly remained around Clara's bed. When Clara went
out, she wound the cat around her neck, like a fur boa. The cat
enjoyed curling around Clara's neck.

Cats often arrived in the zone by "air mail," when the resi-
dents of the surrounding area, wanting to be rid of their kittens,

threw them over the high barbed wire fence. Many a kitten was injured in its flight over the fence. These were adopted with loving care by the cat lovers, and they quickly improved. Like the human prisoners, the camp cats were unassuming. They made do with what their mistresses took away from their own mouths. Once in a while there would be fish soup for supper. The cat owners ate their soup but picked out the small pieces of fish for their little darlings. Clara did that and her cat's black fur glistened. Occasionally the cat, looking for a change, jumped into my bed to sleep. Then immediately Clara scolded him and transferred him to her own bed, so badly did she long for something of her own.

One day, unexpectedly, Clara sat down beside me. I was sitting in the sun, knitting. She asked me to let her inspect the pattern. I gladly showed it to her, and she expressed a desire to learn to knit. I said I would be happy to teach her. During these times together, we talked about recent events. We discussed the administration's campaign against cats, and I told Clara about the spotted tomcat Istihrej who clawed the supervisor's arms and legs when she stuffed him into a sack. The administration did not like Istihrej's constant loud meowing, so they decided to wreak vengeance upon all cats. The prisoners delighted to see their pets disappear as soon as the cat catchers, the supervisor and the two overseers, arrived. Only Istihrej was caught. The poor creature was pushed into a sack, carried to the gate, and given to the soldiers of the guard to beat to death. The dead cat was carried back into the zone to serve as a warning. Istihrej had been the pride and joy of Grandma Petrovna who fed the tom for three years and grew quite attached to him. Now great tears rolled down the old woman's cheeks. When the cat had been buried and the mourners left, a young female cat named Musja sat by the lonely grave for a long time. Only a few months later the soldiers caught and tortured her to death.

We spoke of other topics besides cats. "Once before you said that your mother lost two at once, you and your brother. Where is your brother now?"

"We were tried at the same time. My brother got a death sentence. I got twenty-five years."

"And you think your brother was shot?"

Istihrej (Russian printed newspaper text Resources of the state)

"Yes, of course, what else?"

An uncomfortable silence ensued. Neither of us could find the right words to continue. Suddenly Clara spoke. "My brother was older than I, so all the responsibility for the crimes fell on him. I was a minor then, and nobody listened to me."

"They did not listen, but they gave you twenty-five years."

"Ah, yes. Everybody got long sentences in 1941. The war started, they needed officers, and here we were killing them off. It all began much earlier," Clara recollected. During the Great Purge of Stalin in 1937 they shot my father. He was a gifted scientist, often sent abroad to participate in conferences. I was only eleven when he was shot, my brother was five year older. I will never forget that day. When mother told us, my brother and I went upstairs to father's room and locked the door. My brother took a photograph of our father out of his desk drawer. Striking a solemn pose, he raised two fingers toward the ceiling and recited some words, then made me raise my fingers and repeat what he had said. It was an oath that we would avenge our father. Then I did not fully understand. One day, four years later, my brother asked, 'Do you remember our oath? Now is the time to do something about it.' In the evening, when it began to grow dark, we quietly left the house. My brother explained that it was his duty to kill certain officers whom he heard were to blame in our father's death. Several evenings, we wandered the same streets searching for them. About a week later, a drunken officer stumbled from one of the houses. My brother ordered me to stay on the street to warn him of approaching danger. He followed the officer whom he identified and stabbed to death. We found the next one a few days later, but in his hurry and excitement, my brother only wounded him. He survived. The court sentenced by brother to death but took pity on me as a minor, giving me twenty-five years and placing me in a camp for minors."

Engrossed in the tragic story of Clara's family I had not noticed the approach of a thunderstorm. The dark cloudy sky underlined the sense of catastrophe. I gave an involuntary start at the first flash of lightning and roar of thunder. Clara and I went into the dining hall as the raindrops started to fall. It was an hour until dinnertime and no one was in the hall. We sat on a bench by the window in silence, then I asked, "But was your case considered political?"

"No, it was a common criminal case. I was sentenced under the political paragraph five years ago."

"How long were you in the minor's camp?"

"As long as my age allowed. When I turned sixteen, they sent me to Kalima. Others without papers gave the wrong age and remained with the minors."

"Is it better there?"

"You bet! The food is better, half a glass of milk a day."

"Now I hear you are considered a minor till eighteen."

"That was true then also, but my long sentence was why they sent me sooner. Actually, I escaped from prison twice. The second time, I made it and spent almost half a year on the outside."

Our conversation continued, and Clara told me of her second escape attempt.

"That time, I escaped alone. I was on a transport, and jumped from a moving train in Uzbekistan. An old Uzbek woman took me in. She was lonely, took pity on me, and treated me like a daughter. I will never forget her. I was free for six months."

"How did you get out of the train? Didn't they guard you?"

"Yes and no. The cage in which they were transporting me had a damaged lock which I managed to open."

"You said you were free for half a year. How come they found you later, if they couldn't do it within the first month? I thought the most intensive search takes place immediately after an escape."

"That's what I thought too, but it turned out differently."

"I couldn't be on the old woman's back the whole time. I needed food and clothing which I had to look for. I was careful, waiting for twilight, but what can you do if the local inhabitants have been warned? And especially when they all know each other within a radius of hundreds of kilometers. In this village the people never change. They all know each other's family tree way back. The old woman lived in the furthest corner of the village. I could not show myself in the village at all."

"How did they find you?"

"I decided that it was time to look for another place to live, farther away. I went to the railroad station. That's where they got me. Recognized my snout immediately." She said the last words in a challenging tone.

"Clara, don't be angry, but perhaps you could tell me how you acquired a daughter. You told me that your mother took her in. If I understood correctly, your daughter was born in prison."

"That's a long story," Clara replied unwillingly.

"You can make it shorter," I suggested.

"In Kalima, when I was barely sixteen they transferred me from the minor's to the adult camp. They took me to one of the largest camps in Kalima with several thousand prisoners. There everything was controlled by the thieves, the administration had no say whatsoever. Their main concern was to guard us and get us to work. That's where I got married."

"What do you mean, married?" I exclaimed. "You don't mean to tell me that you had a marriage registry in camp!"

"A marriage of thieves was the law there, and that's enough."

"Who was your groom?"

"He was the ataman of the camp thieves. A 'cossack chieftain.'"

"That sounds altogether romantic," I smiled.

"Romantic? There was so much romance it would make your hair stand on end. Imagine, it was only my second week in camp. Every morning there was a check in the work zone when everybody lined up, men on one side of the road, and women on the other. The overseers on duty made the rounds. All of a sudden, a big, burly fellow stepped out of the men's lineup and approached us, his eyes flaming. All of us sensed trouble. We all held our breath as he came to the women's side and stopped in front of one woman. She was as beautiful as a fairy princess. Seeing him, the beauty went white as chalk. He came up close to her and said, 'Get what you have coming, bitch!' and with one lunge cut her throat. The beautiful woman fell backwards into the sand. As she fell her blood splashed those nearby. Panic erupted."

"And what did the man do?"

"He bent over his victim and closed her eyes which had remained open. Then he said in a hushed voice,

'Forgive me, dear!' and returned to his place in the lineup as though nothing had happened. He stood there and waited."

"And the overseers, what did they do?"

"They came, counted us, looked at the woman on the ground, and left."

"Didn't they say anything?"

"What was there to say? That was not the worst they had seen. Every so often someone would be launched into eternity."

"But they must have found out why he did it."

"There was nothing to find out. She had been his wife and was caught being unfaithful, not with another prisoner but with the chief of the operating division. According to the law of the thieves, that is an unforgiveable offense, punishable by death. If he had not killed her, he would have lost face. This was more than a matter of thieves' traditions. In the corrective labor camps of the Soviet Union, the prisoners' greatest hatred is directed at the chiefs of the operating divisions who recruit informers. They threaten people of weak character and ones with minor offenses, in order to get them to inform on others."

"And then, what happened?"

"Nothing. The commander and the doctor came, ordered the corpse carried off, wrote a protocol, and scratched the dead woman's name off the records."

"I wasn't asking about that. What did they do about the ataman?"

"Oh, they called a trial and sentenced him to additional years for committing the crime in camp. Otherwise everything was the same."

"And he can go on murdering?"

"Sure, why not?"

"I guess people like him can only get out by escaping."

"That's true. About a week later, at dinnertime, we used to eat in three shifts then, I'm eating. That thug who did his wife in comes to my table and says, 'Little one, you're to be my wife now.'"

"Weren't you scared?"

"I was petrified. In the evening I told the older women. All of them, as one, persuaded me to accept and say nothing. I received all kinds of advice. In the end, I submitted to my fate. I was not independent in those days, others did my thinking for me."

"Well I suppose you could say that this proposal was an honor."

"The older women said it was a great honor for me. A wedding day was set. The wedding took place in the men's barracks. They had food and even vodka. I guess it was like a real wedding. I wouldn't know since I've never been to a wedding," Clara commented simply.

"What did the administration do?"

"They had no business sticking their noses into such things, or there could be blood. On such occasions, they pretend to see nothing."

"How old was your husband?"

"He was thirty-two then."

"Twice as old as you. And how long did you celebrate this prison wedding?"

Helene Celmina

"It was a Sunday. We started in the morning, and by the evening the party was over."

"And did you see each other much after the wedding?"

"We saw each other every day in the work zone. Once he came up to me and said, 'Don't go in to dinner, wait for me by the fireman's barrel.' He met me there, then walked ahead and made me follow. He took me to a corner where manure was piled next to the stables. There were several piles of manure with lots of space in between them. There he ordered me, 'Lie down!' My 'wedding night' was spent in the manure, at twelve noon. Frightened, I understood little of what was happening. All I knew was that I better do what I was told. He never talked to me, just issued orders. I realize how innocent I was. At home, they never spoke about marriage or childbirth. I didn't even know I was pregnant. When I felt something moving in my belly, I went to the medical center for hookworm medicine. They gave it to me, no questions asked. More and more often I went for the worm medicine because the movement in my belly was getting stronger. My stomach was getting bigger and bigger with the 'hookworm,' but the medicine did no good. I worried about worms until the day my daughter was born."

"Surely the medics and the doctors must have seen that you were expecting a child."

"I suppose they did, but they used my ignorance. Otherwise, they would have had to release me from hard labor from the sixth month on and give me extra rations. They never gave them to me."

"Then you must have given birth in the camp, not even in the hospital."

"Right there, in the camp medical center."

"And your husband, what about him?"

"I never saw him again because they took me and the child to a mother's camp. Then, after my mother took the little girl, I was brought to the Kemerov District."

"In all this time, you've never heard about him?"

"Oh, yes. I know that he was stupidly killed in a brawl with a knife."

"How do you know for sure that it was he?"

"His nickname was well known among the thieves. I heard from several sources."

"You have a grown up daughter. Would you like to see her?"

"Of course. Does she want to see me, is the question. She is being brought up differently. I don't even know if she has been told who her mother is or even if I exist. What do I have in common with either my mother or my daughter, both fine ladies? My mother is a doctor, and my daughter is probably at a university too."

These forlorn last sentences made me regret my nosiness. A mother's feelings do not wither but burgeon in hard times. Clara's life was so crippled that she must start completely anew. But how? A girl of a good and educated family, she became mixed up with thieves and murderers at sixteen, spent her adolescence among them and learned to view life through their eyes. Their laws and morality and hatreds became Clara's. Who was to blame? Circumstances? The system? If Clara's father lived, Clara would not have spent twenty-five years in prison, and her brother would not have been condemned to death.

Brother and sister did not kill from evil and depravity, but from vengeance. They did not touch the pockets of the officers they killed. They wanted nothing but to avenge their father as they swore as children. Their mistake was not to have talked to their mother or some other adult who could have stopped them. They rushed like crickets into the ashes, and one of them had to burn.

As an adolescent, Clara did not know the value and substance of life, but swam with the current into which she had fallen. As the wife of the ataman, she gained self respect. Perhaps her naive intelligence urged Clara in the later years to find out about life beyond the camp fences.

At times, one was amazed that, imprisoned for twenty-four years, she learned so much. In middle age, she received an added sentence under the clause of anti-Soviet agitation, because she occupied herself too much with politics and incited the other prisoners against the Soviet order. In the last four years, Clara turned to religion. In the Vladimir Prison she met a revivalist who explained the gospels and the existence of God to her. Clara listened with rapture. Faith in God gave Clara's tortured soul balance. After serving twenty-five years, Clara was released in the fall of 1966. I know nothing further of her life.

CHAPTER 18

MURDERERS

A criminal in a forced labor camp is viewed as working off his sentence for breaking social norms. When this criminal criticizes the Soviet system, government or its members, his sentence is immediately increased. Criticism of the Soviet system occurs most often when a thief or murderer, fed up with everything around him, writes a slogan on a wall. This typical graffiti consists of rude words dedicated to the Party and the state. The criminal is subsequently taken to another camp, for those "guilty of especially dangerous crimes against the state." Those originally sentenced for "especially dangerous crimes against the state" are never overjoyed about the arrival of these new prisoners. The newcomers are usually loud, unruly, rude, and unpredictable. Camp #17-A had a number of such women criminals placed there for writing anti-Soviet graffiti on the walls. Mildly put, they were horrible.

It is said that nobody is born a criminal. However, considering Valya Ushakova, it is difficult to understand how one could become like her. A slightly built, middle-aged woman, Valya was neither bad-looking, nor pretty, but her eyes made her always appear angry. Even when she laughed, her eyes stayed angry. Her laughter was harsh, since continuous smoking had made her voice coarse and hoarse.

The paragraph under which she received her twenty-five year sentence was original. She had no rights to parole. She was sentenced for murder and cannibalism. Cannibalism was never prevalent in Russia. Anyone who knew the paragraph under which she was sentenced wanted to know more. Valya did not consider what she did unusual, everything occurred so naturally. Perhaps her reasons for committing the crime lay in Soviet social problems and the low standard of living at that time; perhaps she acted simply for personal gain. According to Valya, there was nothing to eat in the district around the Volga river. People were paying exorbitant prices for food. A loaf of bread cost one hundred rubles on the black market. A worker's average monthly wages were about one thousand rubles, a secretary's about four-hundred-and-fifty. Valya herself had no money to buy bread, presumably since she would not work hard for nominal pay. She discovered a solution to her financial problems and the high cost of food.

Valya had a girl friend. The two of them met often, and the friend spent the night at Valya's place now and then. Valya figured that nobody would immediately miss the girl. One night Valya acted. She killed her friend in order to sell her meat. To dress human meat so that it could be sold without being recognized required hard work. Valya chopped her friend into little pieces which she turned into mince meat using a hand mincer. This took several days.

It is difficult to visualize a young girl like Valya, twenty at that time, carrying out such a cold-blooded task. From the ground meat she made hamburgers which she took to the railroad station to sell. The hamburgers were snapped up almost the moment she appeared with her basket. Who could imagine what kind of hamburgers they were eating? Would anybody believe it? Chances are they would think it was horse meat. Everybody wants to eat, especially where there is little or no food. Her business was thriving. However, people started looking for the girl friend earlier than Valya anticipated. The pressure and the rush of her work left her no time to finish burning her girl friend's bones. Also her neighbors wondered how Valya could be selling hamburgers by the basketful. The militia raided Valya's place while she was mincing her girl friend's last remains, which she planned to sell the next day. Valya was caught with the evidence at the scene of her crime. Asked by the judge why she did it, Valya answered, "For money."

Valya worked in the camp laundry, washing the guards' clothes. In the camps working in the laundry is a privilege. Whenever the soldiers came by horse-drawn wagon to pick up the laundry, Valya brought tea. Whenever there is tea, friendships flourish. In Camp #17-A a number of women criminals in addition to Valya formed eternal friendships by means of tea. Valya, despite having been sentenced for murder, made another friend in camp.

Differences arise among friends, regardless of social circles.

Some difficulty arose between Valya and her girl friend, who normally spent their free time together. Now the two friends kept their distance for two days. In order to spite her friend, Valya asked another criminal in the camp to tea, and spent the whole evening with her. This was a great test for her friend who, the next morning, failed to report for work in the factory. Instead, she did her washing. The hot water came from the boiler stoked by Valya. To prove to Valya how much she had been wronged, the friend took a whole basinful of boiling water and, making sure that Valya watched, dumped it on her own legs. She kept her stockings on since burns obtained this way are much more severe than those on bare legs. The girl friend calculated everything to regain Valya's attention. Valya felt guilty and looked after her friend with care during her long convalescence. As far as one could tell, Valya was happy. She looked after her friend, sharing strong tea with her at night, and life continued as before.

The case of another murderer, Anya Vishnevskaya was different. Anya was alone, with no friends. First, Anya was an ugly woman with a broad freckled face, low forehead and pale, fish-like eyes. Second, she was always angry at somebody and walked up and down the zone cursing in the foulest language. Third, Anya's past made life in the camp difficult. Anya had been sentenced for twenty-five years for murder. A young and healthy woman, she was assigned to felling trees in her first labor camp. She worked under inhuman conditions in the forests. One cold winter day, during a non-stop blizzard, Anya asked the man in charge to stop the work. He refused. Anya then lifted her ax in both hands and, before he could move, struck his head killing him. Anya described this episode as if she was describing the chopping down of a tree. For this new murder, ten years were added to her sentence and she was taken away to another camp.

In the new camp Anya made a friend. They remained close until a new woman, also in for murder, arrived in the camp. The friend then became unfaithful to Anya. Unable to forgive her girl friend for being unfaithful, she went to the woodshed to fetch the ax. Ax in hand, she approached her friend's bedside. The friend leaped up and stared at Anya in surprise. Anya advanced slowly and, when close enough, swung the ax right into the middle of her friend's head. Anya smiled as she spoke.

Anya Vishnevskaya

For greater effect she added, "And her brains spattered all over the wall!" Having said this, Anya's face screwed up into a broad happy smile, revealing her ugly and prematurely blackened front teeth.

Anya told her story after two inmates were released, based on petitions for parole which I wrote. Bored with twenty-three years in camps, Anya decided that it was time to return to the free world. Life in previous camps was more entertaining and time passed quickly. After writing the anti-Soviet curse on a wall, she found life among nuns difficult. She wanted me to write for her exactly the same "piece of paper" I wrote for those who were allowed to go home. As cautiously as possible I reminded her that since her case was more complicated then anyone else's, I was not sure what to write. She had to agree that three bodies and a political curse were actual crimes. Evasively, I said I would think about how to write a plea for her.

A happy Anya appeared the next day in the working space that I was given to prepare drawings and posters. With her repulsive face twisted into a smile, she said, "I like you. Let's be friends!" I felt my blood turn to ice. Anya smiled and came closer. I remained quiet, watching her every move. All of a sudden, she stuck her hand into her pocket and stood, smiling. Abruptly she yanked out her hand, stretched it out over my table and put down a gift, a small compact. Apparently there was no reason to fear she might hurt me. She believed I could help her get out of the camp. I worried that she might warmly embrace and kiss me. I quickly suggested, "Sit down please, Anya. I've thought of what to write." She sat down facing me, and waited.

"Tell me Anya, do you have parents?"

"No, I don't have parents, but I do have relatives."

"Would this relative let you stay at his place for a while, once you left here?"

"He would take me in all right, I know it," Anya announced, sounding as if she had already arranged everything with him.

"Then I'll write that paper stating that you want to stay at your relative's, a Soviet officer's place."

"You're sure good at everything," Anya exclaimed happily.

"And now Anya, go and get some rest, because whenever I'm writing something important, I need to concentrate. Just give me the facts about your family, your birth and court cases." I wrote down everything she told me.

When the plea was ready we went together to the chief administrator's room. She appeared surprised, looked at me with a strange half-smile and, not knowing what else to say, stated briefly, "Good, I'll send it on."

I never expected this criminal to get a parole. However, after about six months, notice came that she would leave if her final plea expressed deep regret for having killed three persons and more important, regret for having written the political curse. The final result turned out positive. I don't know how much joy Anya felt over regaining her freedom. The eyes of the camp inmates conveyed the genuine and true joy they felt at her leaving. Anya kept the women in such a state of constant fear that everyone gave her wide berth and gave in to her demands. Anya threatened several women who dared argue with her promising that their stay in this world would end abruptly. No one doubted that she could fulfill her threat.

Even the camp administrator was scared of Anya and always tried to say a word of appreciation especially when Anya was in a bad mood. Once the commander even fled the camp, using the excuse that she had forgotten something. There was a good reason for her flight since the neighboring camp received several criminals from a clique of inmates separated after serious troubles in the Kemerova district. An ugly incident took place there when the inmates chopped off the head of the camp commander and played soccer with the head until the arrival of the Army. Some of the soccer players were brought to camp #17, across the road from us. In the evenings, Anya yelled out to these new prisoners.

It is difficult to understand people like Valya, Anya, and others sentenced for murder. Up to a certain point they felt rapport for one another, but beyond that they were unpredictable. Every now and then there would be another murder, not because of any special hatred, but from boredom. In men's camps it was a popular pastime to play cards for people's lives with the loser having to kill the first person to come around the corner.

CHAPTER 19

WORK IN THE FIELDS

In the corrective labor camp only the extremely sick and Group I disabled were exempt from work. A Group I disabled is incapable of looking after herself, unable to hold a spoon to feed herself. There was in camp #17-A a young woman who had to be spoonfed by her co-religionists. She was suffering from a heart valve disorder, but Group I status was not granted her because the administration wanted her to have an operation. She refused the operation because as a Jehovah's Witness she could not accept blood transfusions. She had Group II status, even though in this particular case her official status did not matter, she was bedridden. Rarely could she leave her bed for more than a short while. Four women carefully put her on a blanket and, holding the corners, carried her to the door of the bathhouse.

Over half the women in camp #17-A were Group II disabled because of age, not sickness. They stoked the furnaces with coal or worked in the bathhouse. Those whose legs were affected and could not move without help worked in bed. They knotted nets from yarn and string. These old and sickly women made net shopping bags which the camp administration sold to stores. Some of the older women without relatives were happy to learn this new craft, with which they could support themselves after leaving camp.

The greedy camp administration decided that the old women could also tie woolen rugs and thus increase the camp's profit. Finally the idea had to be given up since none of the women possessed enough strength.

The Group III disabled had various chronic and acute diseases which limited their capacity for work. I was a Group III disabled because of stomach ulcers. Invalids in this category were taken under armed guard to the fields to perform varied tasks, depending on the season. In the spring, cabbages had to

191

be planted. Seedlings were grown under glass in the camp. Eaten every day of the year, cabbages are the staple food in prisons. Even though the prisoners grow, harvest, and preserve the cabbages, the state charges for them.

The cabbage fields were enormous. The portion of the field to be worked on a particular day was marked with wooden signs saying "No entry. Forbidden zone." Every morning before going to the fields, the prisoners lined up by the gates to allow the female guard to check underneath their black uniform dresses for colored clothing. This was to prevent escapes, since black clothing identified them as prisoners. The prisoners were then counted and their identity cards collected. Every prisoner, including the bedridden, has a special card with a photo, giving her name, length of sentence, and the paragraph under which

The column moving

the sentence has been passed. These cards allow the administration to know where every prisoner is at any moment. Before
the gates opened, a guard said "morning prayers," that is, gave
orders to march in closed columns, to obey all commands, not
to converse, not to leave the column. Prisoners disobeying
would be shot without warning.

Then, slowly the column started to move. Those who had
trouble walking were placed in front to ensure that there
would be no stragglers and that the column moved in an
orderly fashion. The village through which we passed every
day had no discernable road, only dark gray sand without a
blade of grass, not even a dandelion. The lack of greenery
looked unnatural, however it resulted from the collective
scratching of the villagers' hens and pigs.

On the way to work the column moved slowly to shorten
the actual working period. Returning from work, these same
women who in the morning barely dragged themselves along,
marched with such a lively step that one wondered where all
this energy came from. On reaching the field, the prisoners
squatted on the ground till the warning signs were in place.
Then two of the stronger women carried a little wooden latrine
shed to the middle of the field where a third one dug a hole. A
wooden cask of drinking water was brought to the field in a
horse-drawn wagon. Bread, a mug, and spoon were brought
along by the prisoners themselves. One was also allowed to
bring salt.

Planting cabbages was not difficult. One woman would
walk ahead digging holes with a spade while another placed
the seedlings in the holes. The seedlings were carried to the
fields in nursery boxes and left on the edge of the field. The
hardest task was watering, since water had to be carried from
the river in pails. Although the river adjoined one side of the
field, the other side of the field was a long way off. The watering
was done in shifts.

Lunch, such as it was, was brought to the fields in large
metal containers. Sitting on the ground to eat was fine when it
wasn't raining and the soil was dry. However, fights broke out
when the guards ordered the prisoners to sit in the mud. During
rain, dark water from the wet hems of the women's black
dresses ran down their bare legs coloring them black. Only during prolonged rainy periods did work in the fields cease.

Once it rained for a whole week. Since the soil of Mordovia is mostly clay and could not absorb all that water, little lakes formed in the low lying areas and remained for several days. Some of the roads on which we walked to work were flooded. The women holding their dresses high, looking like ostriches, slowly moving through the water, presented a strange sight. The cold water reached to the knees or higher on the bare-footed women, but the guards wore high rubber boots. In one place the water was so deep that the women were ferried across by tractor, and later, when the water subsided a little, by horse-drawn wagon. Several fields of cabbages were also flooded and in the sky-blue water the heads of the cabbages looked like tiny islands arranged in neat and orderly rows.

Much of the summer was spent thinning and weeding sugarbeets. Sugarbeet tops were our best meal, far tastier than sauerkraut soup. We carried the tops back to the camp zone as well. Sometimes we were allowed to carry the tops into camp and sometimes not, in which case they were left to wilt on the ground by the camp gate. The recipe for cooking sugarbeet tops was simple; the tops were rinsed, torn into pieces, and sprinkled with salt. Hot water was poured over the tops and breadcrumbs stirred into the resulting broth, to produce a meal fit for the gods.

Once I worked for a few days thinning red beets. Like most beginners, I pulled out weeds and smaller plants, leaving the larger ones to grow. The more experienced women taught me to pull the larger ones and leave the little ones. Working with the red beets provided a daily feast of at least ten beets the size of radishes. We also ate the beet tops and tried to bring them back for friends in the camp.

A successful propaganda campaign against us women prisoners had been carried out in the criminal men's camp where our food was cooked. Often we met these men, escorted by guards and dogs, as they walked to work in the fields. The men's eyes expressed hatred. They swore at us, adding to every filthy swear word that beloved Russian adjective "fascist." Sometimes we walked close to the black-clad males who became especially aggressive, throwing lumps of dried clay. On those occasions the guards looked away, pretending to see nothing. Only the dogs barked in confusion. Considering the fact that Russian males have an inordinate interest in women and seek desparately to talk to any women around, the men's behavior proved that they had been told unimaginably horrible things about us.

Only two young male convicts were not hostile. They were trustees, unguarded, who drove wagons transporting various necessities, including our drinking water. Trustees are criminals not convicted of serious theft, rape, or similar offences; usually trustees have been convicted for non-payment of alimony, disturbing the peace, vandalism, or other petty crimes.

One of the men, Kolya, had drawn a two year sentence for fighting in a public place, in front of a restaurant. He was in the restaurant with a girl whom two other males also found attractive. The two strangers grabbed at the girl. Kolya beat up both of her unwelcome admirers.

Kolya brought us our tools and our luncheon soup. Sometimes he secretly threw down a handful of green onion tops which he gathered to make our soup more palatable. On those occasions he winked so we would know in which direction to look for this delicacy. Kolya was not allowed to talk to us. Nevertheless he sometimes drove his cart near enough that we could exchange a few words. Once his horse appeared out of control close to me. Scared of the horse, I jumped away noticing at the same time something falling off the cart. Everyone, even the guards, watched the horse while I saw two cucumbers and a bunch of green onions. Not knowing how I deserved this kindness, my joy was indescribable. Nevertheless my first thought was "who is on guard duty tonight?" because I now faced the problem of getting at least one cucumber into the camp to share with someone else. Giving provides joy. In a place visited by joy only rarely, all opportunities to give must to be seized with alacrity. I decided to smuggle only one cucumber into camp. While continuing to work, I turned my back on the guards and swiftly and unobtrusively consumed one of my precious cucumbers. To look for salt would have made me too conspicuous.

During the working day my cucumber and onion tops remained hidden in a little heap of weeds and beet tops. Shortly before leaving for the camp I knelt and gathered up my hidden goodies. I hid the cucumber in the front of my dress. That evening, because there was a fairly decent guard on duty, I hoped that I would not be searched down to my skin. I placed the onion tops on my sleeve which I rolled up. Nothing showed, and I felt confident of getting them into camp. I openly carried the beet tops in my hand. Arriving at the camp we lined up in fours, waiting for the guards to check us in. There was no serious search, the guards merely looked into our food satchels, counted us, opened the gate and let us in. My smuggling operation was successful!

All able-bodied women worked in the clothing factory and had no opportunities to acquire fresh food to alleviate the monotony of cabbage soup and porridge. Thus my fresh cucumber brought great enthusiasm and even greater amazement because everyone knew cucumbers did not grow in the beet fields. I gave the cucumber to Zelma who gave half to another friend. The onion tops I divided among three people, who probably divided them again, down to one stalk per person. Since beet tops were easy to obtain we handed them out right and left. This was our way to store up vitamins for the winter when there was no fresh food of any kind available.

Some prisoners received money from home with which they ordered Soviet newspapers and magazines which contained mostly communist propaganda. No matter how much money a prisoner had, there were no opportunities to buy a fresh apple or even a single lettuce leaf. Had the prisoners been allowed to keep their money, they might have bribed the guards to bring vegetables into camp from the village store. However the money was kept by the camp cashier.

Judging by conversations among the guards the village store stocked little besides liquor. When we walked to work through the center of the village we could see what the villagers bought in the store. Cotton net shopping bags are universally used throughout Russia. Except for Moscow and other large cities, nothing is wrapped in Russia. Unwashed potatoes are thrown together with bread and other baked goods, while salt herrings are simply carried in one's hand.

Once an open potato wagon stood by the village store. The guards did not notice it in time to take the women across the street. The women in our camp were not thieves, most of them were deeply religious. Nevertheless every one fell on the wagon and grabbed at least two potatoes. The guards threatened to shoot, but without an official order they couldn't. The imprisoned women knew that survival depends on learning how to feed themselves. The shouts of the guards were no more effective than the yapping of puppies. When a guard raised his voice and started to abuse the prisoners, the women yelled back. It was useless trying to scare those who have been threatened for years.

For a whole week we hoed the onion fields. This was an extremely pleasant job for various reasons. To begin with, the road to the onion fields led past fields of carrots. The guards' shouts and threats were ignored as every woman leaped into the carrot field to pull out as many carrots as possible. In the onion fields we ate as many onions as we wanted, and hid the onion tops in our clothing. The main challenge was to smuggle whole onions into the camp for friends. A teacher from Lithuania was especially clever in this maneuver. For several days she carried onions into camp for those who needed them most. But the day arrived when her smuggling was discovered. To everyone's surprise the female guard went straight to the teacher and pulled onions from her hair, one after the other, six in all. We wondered how the guard discovered the onions so easily. Perhaps one of the prisoners observed the teacher removing the onions and, resentful that none was offered to her, betrayed the teacher.

To prolong the feast of the onions everyone worked as slowly as possible. The fields were cared for with extreme love, so that even the tiniest weed did not escape. The work norms in the fields were so unrealistic that even with the best effort we could never fulfill them. Thus we didn't try and consequently never received pay. Our recompense was what we could eat and bring into camp; the sunshine and fresh air were treasures by themselves. Even though the field workers were invalids we actually looked healthier, bronzed by the sun and wind, than those who spent long days at their sewing machines in the clothing factory.

Our greatest pay for the summer's work came at fall harvest. In the spring any green shoot by the roadside was valuable, while in the summer the sugarbeet tops were treasured. By the fall the beet tips lost their value. Cucumbers were harvested first. They were delicious eaten in the fields, and were nearly impossible to smuggle into camp. The guards asked the escorting soldiers where we had worked that day. If we worked with sugarbeets, the guards did not bother to search us, but if we worked with onions, cucumbers, or other valuable vegetables, the search was thorough. One way to frustrate the search was to wrap a small cucumber in a handkerchief and hold it in one's hand. During the search one raised one's arms, still holding the cucumber, and the guard ran her hands over one's body without finding anything.

Kolya transported the harvested cucumbers to the village store where the camp guards and administrators bought them by the sackful. The cucumbers were pickled and eaten until the following spring. There isn't a Russian village home that does not have row upon row of wooden casks containing pickled cucumbers and sauerkraut. Cucumbers and cabbages are grown near every camp. While the prisoners are fed cabbage every day of the year, they are never given any cucumbers.

The heads of cabbages grow enormous in Russia, especially since there are no pests, not even a single cabbage moth. Usually the cabbages are sliced with a special cutter and salted in a medium-size wooden cask. A few chopped carrots or cranberries are added. For prisoner consumption the cabbages are chopped with an ax, like firewood. The pieces are thrown into an enormous vat buried in the ground. The heavier women, wearing special long rubber boots, sprinkle salt on the cabbages and stomp them down. It is impossible to clean the huge vat properly. The remains of the past year's sauerkraut lends a bad taste to the sauerkraut in winter, but in autumn nobody worries about it.

The greatest feast was harvesting the potatoes. The potato fields were large and the harvesting usually lasted three weeks. Potatoes could be eaten raw, after cleaning them with a piece of glass and adding a little salt. Some guards allowed us to build a fire, and then we baked the potatoes. Smuggling the potatoes into the camp, however, remained a problem. During the potato harvest the searches at the camp gates were especially stringent. Once a woman imprisoned for religious offences was found with a whole stockingful of potatoes tied underneath her dress. Her potatoes were confiscated and she was punished by having to sort rags in the clothing factory several days.

Other women baked the potatoes, peeled and mashed them into their drinking mug which every field worker carried. Usually the mugs were not confiscated. Only when the guard was feeling especially ornery would she throw the white mashed potatoes into the dark soil, thus demonstrating her power.

While the rest of the harvest was counted by the sackful, potatoes were weighed by the bushel basket. Every full basket contained ten kilograms of potatoes, and everyday I stood on the platform of a heavy truck hauling up and emptying about one thousand baskets of potatoes. During the potato harvest everyone went to the fields to eat, even if they could hardly work. Thus the amount of work varied: Some picked a great many baskets while some barely gathered ten during the day. There were rest periods while the potatoes were trucked to sorting sheds.

On one occasion I carried watercolors and paper to the field. When fall cast a golden glow over the landscape the desire to paint was irresistible. There were woods on two sides of the potato field. Between the field and the woods were narrow strips of meadow on which several dozen haystacks stood. The haystacks belonged to the families of the guards, each of which kept a cow. These haystacks, lit by the afternoon sun were lovely. Behind the haystacks was a thick grove of young, dark green spruce, among which the yellow tops of a few birches stood out. In front of the spruce grew white birch trees, and the haystacks were surrounded by a fence of thin white birch saplings. A rich and beautiful autumnal landscape.

The rest periods weren't long, and my watercolor was finished in about twenty minutes. The truck returned as I was adding the last shadows to the foot of the haystacks. I put my colors and the still-wet painting on the grass to dry and returned to my job. When the evening came and I was too exhausted to continue lifting the baskets, the guards allowed another woman to help me. This day, a jeep arrived out of which stepped the commander of the guard of all the nearby camps, the chief of operations and two other officers. Such a procession was never seen before and work slowed down considerably.

Our escort that day was Yuri Kashirski and a soldier from the regular Army. Kashirski spoke to the officers. He pointed to me. Every officer looked in my direction and I strained to hear what Kashirski was saying: " . . . she fixed this area with absolute precision and I therefore considered it my duty to report it. Imagine the consequences if a plan of this strategically important object was secretly conveyed to the Pentagon!"

The officers approached and asked to see what I drew that day. Greatly puzzled I came down from the truck platform, went to the edge of the field, picked up my now-dry watercolor which I handed to the chief of operations. He looked at it casually and demanded to see the other drawings I made that day. I explained that this was the only one. The officers took another look at the watercolor of the seven haystacks, five birches, and a grove of spruces. Of course the chief of operations, convinced that I was hiding something, did not believe me.

He called Kashirski and asked him: "What did that drawing look like?" stressing the word "that." Kashirski looked at me with his only good eye, and said fawningly that this was it. The boss took the drawing nearer to Kashirski and asked him to take another look. Again Kashirski confirmed that this was the only painting I made that afternoon. "But this is just an ordinary landscape," said one of the officers. Kashirski tried to explain that it wasn't ordinary at all: the barracks housing the soldiers doing guard duty were near, while behind the village were three large prison zones, and on the other side of the woods were the kennels where guard dogs were bred. The painting would allow the Pentagon to ascertain the exact location of these strategically important objects. I suppressed laughter as it occurred to me that maybe Kashirski, suffering from heat stroke, lost his wits.

The chief of operations curtly stated that he saw no such thing in the drawing, returned it to me, exchanged glances with the other officers and marched back to the jeep. When they were in the jeep, everyone laughed. Obviously one of the officers said something sarcastic about Kashirski. Then the jeep sped toward the village center, leaving a cloud of gray dust behind. It was time to stop work. Quickly we emptied the last baskets of potatoes, gathered the food satchels with our spoons and mugs, formed a column and walked back to camp. Kashirski slunk along at the rear of the column like a dog with his tail between his legs.

That incident was talked about for days in the camp. Every prisoner wanted a good look at the "strategically important" watercolor. The watercolor became so popular that later in the winter I made an oil painting of it which I hung up. The story spread in the village also. Several female guards, laughing at Kashirski, pointed out their own haystacks in the painting and named the owners of the other haystacks.

After the harvest, the potatoes were sorted. The camps

were contracted to deliver a portion of the harvest to the state. The large potatoes were stored in huge cellars, the small ones, used to feed the prisoners, were covered with straw and soil. Even the invalids in Group II who could barely walk the kilometer to the sorting sheds volunteered. Everyone longed to taste a potato which never appeared in its natural state on the camp menu. For the stronger women, sorting the potatoes was fairly heavy work. The sorted potatoes were put in large wooden chests, each holding one hundred kilograms. The instructions specified that two people should carry the chest to the storage bins. However because invalids could not manage, four carried each chest by the handles. When the potato level rose in the bins to the height of a man, lifting a hundred kilos of potatoes plus the ten kilogram chest was difficult. However working with the potatoes was enjoyable.

Not only people, but the village pigs enjoyed the potato harvest as well. One day a sow with her two piglets arrived at the sorting sheds. The piglets were petted and their backs scratched. When one of the older women lay down on her side to rest during a lunch break, a piglet contentedly cuddled up against her stomach. The woman looked happy because she was the one chosen by the piglet as its "mama."

After the potatoes, the carrots were harvested. Even though everyone worked as slowly as possible because the carrot fields were small, the harvesting was finished in a few days. In order to smuggle the carrots into the camp, we grated them into our drinking mugs. The graters were made from the lid of a tin can in which holes were punched with a nail. The graters passed from hand to hand so that everybody could grate a few carrots into her mug.

Last to be harvested were sugarbeets and the beets used as cattle feed. The cattle feed beets tasted good if eaten with salt and bread. The sugarbeets weren't tasty, and we only ate their tops.

Work in the fields lasted for six months, from May until November. When the harvest was in, my half-year's earnings amounted to twenty-three tiny onions. I put them in a stocking under my bed so that during a casual inspection it could not be seen. The onions were the only supplement to the meager prison fare during the winter months, not only for me but for my friends who had nothing.

CHAPTER 20

MONEY

There probably aren't many modern states whose citizens have never seen their own currency. Yet in camp #17-A several women had never seen Soviet-printed money. After the war they fled into the forests with their husbands, and from the forests they went straight to prison. Other women knew the currency in use right after the war, but were arrested before 1948 when the currency reform brought new bills. In 1961 the bills were changed again and only two of us recognized these latest bills. The rest had neither seen nor handled these bills, and had no idea of current prices. They only knew camp prices which reflected camp values and accounting practices.

For every prisoner the camp accounting department kept a card which displayed the name, length of sentence, and amount of money owned by the prisoner. Income and expenses were recorded on this card. According to Soviet law, prisoners receive only fifty percent of their earnings. The other half is transferred to the state, as its part of the punishment, even though court sentences never mention it. The Soviet Union enriches itself with slave labor, and it profits from keeping people in corrective labor camps.

The well-trained seamstress, provided she fills the high work norms, gets forty rubles booked into her account card, the highest possible income. Most factory workers earned about twenty rubles or less. Those who worked in the fields made ten to fifteen rubles monthly. Then came the deductions, the largest of which were made for food and clothing. The deduction for food was made at the end of each month after calculating the cost of the groats fed to the prisoners. Any difference in the food deduction was due to the price of groats. The bread was always the same, dark, wet, heavy, with a slightly bitter-sour and salty aftertaste, and its price never changed. Nobody knows how much the administration charged for the cabbages which the

Helene Celmina

prisoners grew themselves and ate every day. Deductions were also made for room, light, heat, and bedding.

Having to buy prison clothing was annoying because it fit absolutely no one. One wonders who designed, cut, and stitched these garmets. When prison clothing gets wet, the color runs and blackens the skin. Prison dress is obligatory and cannot be refused, it is handed out and charged for.

One also wonders where the underclothing which prisoners must purchase, is made. There is no reason to suppose that all prisoners are the size of pregnant elephants, but the only underclothing available to the inmates of camp #17-A was that size. We laughed about it and once two of us stepped into a pair of huge cotton pants, and they weren't even tight!

The only article issued that fit was the footwear: lace-up canvas boots with rubber soles. For winter everyone was issued a quilted cotton jacket and a large plaid shawl. The whole issue of prison clothing cost sixty rubles and had to last for two years.

Because I earned so little which did not cover the various deductions, I was not forced to purchase another set of clothing after two years and used the first issue until the end of my sentence. After my release I owed the state fifty-seven rubles and twenty kopeks. I worried that I would be forced to pay this after starting work outside, but I never had to.

CHAPTER 21

MAIL

Mail is eagerly awaited in the camps. With the exception of those few letters and telegrams telling of the death of a relative or other bad news, mail brings great joy to the inmates. In truth, mail is virtually the only link between the prisoners and the outside world.

Sometimes a whole year, or even two, pass before a prisoner is allowed to write to family; before the trial sending or receiving mail is forbidden. After sentencing, the law allows every prisoner to write two letters a month, but only to members of the family. Only if there are no close relatives can a friend's name be put in the prisoner's personal file and permission is obtained from both the judge and the camp administration to correspond with that particular person. No mail is allowed to or from other friends.

All letters to family members must be put in the camp's mailbox, with envelopes unsealed. Because every letter is read by a censor, no letter is ever delivered sooner than a fortnight. All letters from the outside are opened. Sometimes the stamps are removed. However, not even the obliteration of whole sentences with black printer's ink can diminish the joy of hearing from home. Many women serving ten or fifteen year sentences never received one letter. These women either had no family left, or had relatives who never wrote.

Sometimes a happy prisoner, carrying a letter or even several letters meets one of the unfortunate ones who never receive mail, and resolves after release to write letters of encouragement and understanding to her camp acquaintances and friends. Then comes the day of release. Farewells are exchanged between women who, for years have slept, eaten, and worked side by side, suffered cold, pain, and privation together. With many hugs and tears, the one for whom the gateway to freedom opens in ten or fifteen minutes promises: "I'll write to you, to all of you." Sometimes a letter or two arrives, but sometimes the tearful and sincere promise is forgotten as soon as the prison gates close. Occasionally the promise is kept. Some people keep in touch even in freedom, tied by common fate and interests.

Besides letters, relatives also send newspapers, magazines, and books published in the Soviet Union. Material published in satellite countries, Poland or East Germany, is not allowed into the camps. Writing materials, paper, pencils, and even water-colors, can be sent.

Sometimes dear, well-meaning relatives enclose a small bar of chocolate with the magazines and newspapers. Because this is not allowed, the whole packet is returned to the sender. Sometimes a kindly guard can be bribed into keeping the choc-olate for herself and handing over the magazines and newspa-pers to the prisoner. Even sometimes the guard will allow the prisoner to eat the chocolate, but only if there are no witnesses.

Instead of chocolate, sometimes a piece of soap or a tube of toothpaste is enclosed. Then the inmate listened patiently to the reproofs and instructions to advise one's relatives not to send forbidden goods. After the rebuke, the wrapper was removed from the soap, which was carefully scrutinized for hidden writ-ing, the tube of toothpaste examined for illegal enclosures, sender and receiver scolded again and finally, the articles were handed over to the inmate.

Food packages seldom arrived at the camp because they could only be received, and with special permission of the camp administration, after serving half of the sentence. Not everybody merited the permission. Other things could go wrong. Vera, sentenced to seven years, and having served five, should have had the privilege of receiving food parcels from home. A good worker, she had not incurred other penalties. Permission was refused several times on various pretexts, but finally it was granted. Several months later a food parcel arrived, but Vera was not allowed to take it because the sender was not a close enough relation. The fact that Vera grew up in an orphanage because her parents were dead was stated in her personal file. However the distant relative who sent the parcel was not named in the file. In its bureaucratic zeal the adminis-tration returned the parcel because packets from unauthorized senders were not allowed into camp #17-A. Vera's bitter tears were to no avail.

A strange food parcel was sent by a mother to her daughter who already spent more than twenty years in the camps. This parcel was authorized so the daughter could receive it. To everybody's surprise, the parcel contained nothing but sunflower seeds. Russians and sunflower seeds go together like horses and oats. The floors of provincial clubs and theaters are always thickly covered with husks of these seeds which are considered snack food. When some of the inmates expressed their astonishment at this unusual parcel, she explained that her mother is poor and unable to get to Moscow to shop for food. In the country, the only obtainable foodstuff were the sunflower seeds. She was telling the truth, and was happy to receive her parcel which came from a mother with love.

CHAPTER 22

BEDBUGS

Every spring all the barracks were whitewashed inside and out. This was dangerous because the whitewashing was done with lime, which if it gets into the eyes, causes blindness. Splashes of lime corrode bare skin, and these wounds heal slowly.

The well-organized whitewashing was carried out on Sunday, since work for the state was done weekdays. Early in the morning all the bedboards, actually four or five planks nailed together, were taken outside. The younger and stronger women did the whitewashing with tools they made by themselves, as none were provided by the administration. Clumps of last year's grass or old rags cut into thin strips were tied to a stick. This "brush" was dipped into the thin lime solution and banged against the ceiling, covering every nook and cranny.

The older women stayed outside, trying to get rid of the bedbugs in the cracks of the bedboards. It was too difficult to reach the bugs living in the quarters. Often the bugs fell from the ceiling where they lived undisturbed. In desperation a piece of crunched-up paper could be lit and held beside the biggest cracks in the bedboards. Partly burned, the bugs fell crackling onto newspapers or sheets spread beneath the beds. "If one could eat bedbugs like raisins, there wouldn't be one left," joked one woman.

Now during whitewashing to stop the bugs from flourishing some women tended a large pot of boiling water with which all bedboards were scoured. The cracks were probed with knitting needles, and finally filled with softened soap. However, once the soap dried and fell out of the cracks, the bugs had snug living spaces again. Then the sacks of wood shavings which served as mattresses were carefully examined. When the whitewashing inside was finished, ten women quickly scrubbed the floors and the clean beds were taken back inside. The outside walls were whitewashed, and the work was done.

Helene Celmina

After spring cleaning the bugs were bothersome only occasionally. However, by the middle of summer, they multiplied again. Every square meter of the floor area held a body and there was no lack of warm blood. No chemicals against the bugs were provided. The chemicals cost money and prison regulations did not call for them.

CHAPTER 23

CAMP #3

All who have spent time in the Potyma Archipelago of the Mordovian Autonomous Republic know where camp #3 is. All the camps in the Archipelago are connected by a narrow gauge railroad, at the end of which is camp #3, the combined hospital for all camps. One was taken to the hospital only in serious cases, such as operations, pregnancies, or diseases requiring continuous laboratory analysis or x-rays. Naturally toothaches did not qualify for the hospital, regardless of how painful they were. No dental care was provided in camp #17-A. Once in a while, generally during the summer, a dentist would visit. All aching teeth were yanked out and occasionally also those that were not. Because the dentist was there for one day only, there was no time for repairs and fillings. However, if one was taken to camp #3 for laboratory tests or x-rays, one could see a dentist as well. Only the camp doctor could approve a transfer to the hospital, except in cases of sudden serious illness, when the camp's free medical assistant could.

The medic normally accompanied a patient during the transfer to the hospital, in case medical help was needed along the way. The trip was not long, but rough, over a road that was merely a forest clearing filled with potholes and ruts. It seemed amazing that the administration having access to the cheapest labor never thought of constructing a decent dirt track, let alone a paved one. Whenever it rained, the area flooded because the clay soil could absorb no water. Trucks could barely get through the deepest holes. Every now and then the truck would threaten to tip over.

For those sitting inside the windowless compartment, the experience was terrible—no air, tossing around and swaying. Motion sickness is almost inevitable. When the trip is finally over, and one steps out of the truck, the ground seems to continue swaying.

Waiting for the train the prisoners must sit on the ground, regardless of season or whether the ground is dry. Seated prisoners are easier to guard. When the train arrives the prisoners are placed in the cages. The guards on these trains are always "the sons of the steppes" from Central Asia, young men who do not speak Russian, but have been taught to bark out orders.

The hospital is by the railroad. When the train stops, the men are lined up and driven through the gate of the male zone and the women through their gate. When I went the female guards were only interested in the slips that contained our first name, surname, father's name, paragraph, length of sentence, and the number of the camp we came from. After our papers were checked, we, the only three women there, were put into a waiting room. After a long wait, a different guard took us to the hospital block that was also a barracks, where we were placed in the care of a nurse who was a prisoner. She briefly went through the list of clothing allowed. Because of the cold, end-of-November weather, with rain puddles already frozen over, we could keep more than we would have in summertime. We kept footwear, stockings, underwear, head scarf and gloves, if anyone had them. The rest was stored to be returned when we left the hospital. They gave us each a coarse shirt, yellowed from repeated washing, and a gray padded smock. I put on the shirt and was about to pick up the smock when I noticed it was filthy. The other two had already put on smocks equally filthy with caked dirt on the neck and lapels. Without putting on the smock, I stood shivering. The same nurse returned and told me to pick up my clothing and follow her to the store. I asked for a clean smock. The nurse gave me an odd look, and added in a coarse, smoker's voice, "Just think. We've got a lady here! It's good enough for everybody but not for her! We don't have any others."

"If you don't, you don't. But I'm not going to put it on."

"Yes you are. Everyone wears one and so will you!"

"I wouldn't think of it."

"I'll call the guard!"

"Go ahead."

"I don't have time to fight with an oddball like you.
Let's go."

The nurse yanked open the door, the other two grabbed
their things and followed into the yard. I hesitated, then seeing
that it was senseless to fight, I picked up my things and, clad in
the shirt, crossed the yard to the store.

It started to snow. Tiny snowflakes landed on my naked
shoulders and melted, leaving droplets. By the time we reached
the store, I could not give my name, because my teeth were
chattering.

The nurse haughtily explained to the woman in the store,
"This lady doesn't like our clothes. They're too common for
her. She needs them straight from Paris."

The woman shook her head, "Now you cannot please
everybody."

I kept quiet. The second prisoner pretended not to hear anything but the third one observed that the hospital instead of
handing out such dirty smocks, should wash them at least once
a year.

The woman in the store now explained solemnly, "Look
here! We do wash the smocks once a year, each summer. But
who's to blame when we run into pigs that wipe their noses
and behinds on the corners of their smocks? We cannot wash
them more often because we don't have enough soap, nor is
there any place to dry them."

I was now so cold that neither jumping around nor rubbing
my hands together helped. Fortunately, the discussion ended
and nobody paid any more attention to me. The nurse took me
into a large room with about thirty beds and gave me a bed at
the end against a rear wall. I went to bed immediately to coun-
teract the cold. Because the room was warm, I started to thaw
out, with little help from the thin felt blanket. The women lying
nearby asked which camp I was from. Learning that I came
from camp #17-A, they sighed compassionately and fell silent.

Several nurses, both prisoners and free citizens, walked
through the hospital. The free nurses appeared to be too young
to be in a prison hospital. But on the other hand, they were
locals, born and bred right there and were used to prisoners

ever since childhood. The entire neighborhood consisted of forced labor camps and houses for the camp personnel. The local children knew that the best place to work was in the prison camps. The nurses who were prisoners, were all middle-aged. All the orderlies were inmates. Towards the evening, when activity slowed down, I asked a first-aid nurse who seemed more affable than the rest, if I could get a few buckets of hot water.

"What do you want hot water for?"

"I was given a smock which is so dirty!"

"I know, I know. But it's going to be difficult to get the water."

"But this is a hospital isn't it?"

"That's true, but water is a great deficit here. We're lucky to get enough for the kitchen. Washing takes second place."

"Where does one get water?"

"Nowhere, really. The patients carry it from the well. There is water enough there! But we don't have a place to heat it."

"Then it looks like I won't be able to wash my smock."

"It is going to be difficult, but we'll think of something.

Becoming more responsive, she said she would bring me water. The only way to heat it was on the little electric hotplate the nurses used during the day to boil the needles. I thanked her for being so friendly and felt happy, especially after she told me that she, too, couldn't stand the dirty clothes.

The orderly brought two buckets of water. Since there was only one hotplate, I had to wait for the water to heat. To break the silence I asked, "You probably wash your uniforms your-self, don't you?"

"Our own and the doctor's gowns too, because the laundry cannot be trusted. Things are either stolen or replaced with worn out ones. You never get back what you send. Surgical sheets are in special demand."

"Why do they steal the sheets?"

"Embroidery. They're such fanatics that they won't use old sheets. They insist on new ones."

"Yes, I've noticed that the public here gets really carried away with handicrafts."

She asked me what I was in for. I told her briefly and trying to find out why she was here, I asked, "You're suffering for fixing books, right?"

"No, murder," she answered simply.

"I would have never imagined that. You, in for murder!"

"Life's funny. Many don't believe it and think I'm kidding. But it happened, and here I am in jail."

"Did you really kill someone?"

"Yes, my husband," she said with a smile.

"If people don't get along, I would think divorce would be the better answer. Why did you have to kill him?"

"Because he was a bastard but wouldn't give me a divorce. And then, too, there was someone else whom I wanted to marry."

"And he's waiting for you now?"

"I don't know if he's waiting or not. He's locked up for the same thing. We did it together."

"I see . . ." I said thoughtfully, not knowing what to say.

Then she told me her life's story. Her husband seemed to be the devil incarnate. He turned up at her place in the middle of the night, having been released or paroled from jail. She was living with her father. Using threats of violence he forced the father and daughter to wait on him. Because of his size and strength, they were in no position to turn him in to the militia. One night, seeing no other release, she got the despot drunk, and she and her lover killed him. They expected a light sentence. Nevertheless, they each received seven years.

The water heated, and the friendly orderly gave me soap. The water turned muddy as soon as I started washing. A young woman brought a third bucket of water for rinsing. That one bucket had to do since I could not fetch water myself. I hung the smock up to dry outside, where it froze solid. After four days I brought it in and hung it by the stove in the ward, where it finally dried. I patched the places where the padding was falling out. Finally, after six days, I had a decent smock. As a result of walking around in my shirt I contracted bronchitis which lasted for three months.

The Russian women from the surrounding criminal camps complained that because they did so much work, they were both healed and maimed in this hospital. The two orderlies looked after the doctor's offices and the operating rooms. The prisoners could not wash the floors of these rooms because they would steal everything. The floors in the remaining rooms, including the ward, were washed by the hospitalized prisoners, who also fed the stove. The stronger ones fetched the ice cold water from a well while the weaker ones washed the floors and threw the dirty water into the yard. The hospital had no sewers. As a concession to comfort, the dry latrine was equipped with a "throne" made out of boards. Facilities for washing were much worse than in the camp. In camp #17-A each prisoner had her personal wash basin, and for every sixty prisoners there was a common hygiene room. Even with mushrooms growing in the moldy corners of this room, we could brush our teeth and wash our feet. We washed whatever we pleased in our basins as long as we fetched the water ourselves. Here, in the hospital, not every inmate was strong enough to fetch the water. The well was deep and the parapet rose chin high. Furthermore, the handle on the hoist used for winching up the bucket was stiff, especially during the first few turns. Normally two people worked it together.

At that time many inmates could not get out of bed. One was paralyzed and could not speak. These patients were cared for by other inmates. The free nurses only gave injections and handed out the pills prescribed by the doctors, they never washed those confined to their beds. Other inmates now and then brought them a basin of water, enough to wash their hands. Every ten days the inmates, holding each other up, took the long walk to the sauna. This was a sad sight, sick inmates dragging those sicker than themselves. When they finished washing, everybody received a clean shirt but wore the same dirty smock. We were allowed to spend a whole hour in the bath-house, sufficient to get clean enough to last for the next ten days. The only ones who could not manage were those with, as the criminal prisoners said, the bad bourgeois habit of washing every day. Those who wanted to wash daily could take a mug

In a prison hospital all patients must work. (Russian printed newspaper text: Envoy's of the new shift of Communism's builders.)

of tea into the yard, and pour it on their hands. Also those who wanted to brush their teeth badly enough went into the yard.

The only clean place in the primitive hospital was the operating room, which was located in the same barracks as the women's ward and the record rooms. Complicated surgery was carried out in the hospital of camp #3. Intestinal, stomach, and other operations that could not be postponed were done immediately. Heart operations, however, were done in the Leningrad. Camp #3 was known for intestinal and stomach operations. The surgeon gained plenty of experience from the male prisoners who every now and then decided to visit the hospital for an operation. These men went to prison straight from detention homes for the underaged, and subsequently served several terms. Prison was their life. Whenever these professional prisoners desired to rest or to hold hands with the nurses, they swallowed the most unimaginable things, most often small metal objects, but occasionally a spoon or a thermometer. Others proved their originality by swallowing a whole chess or domino set. The prisoner, after explaining what he had done to the administration or to the camp doctor, was taken to the hospital for x-rays. Even the most hardened criminals respected and loved doctors. They knew that by swallowing objects they were risking their lives and were at the mercy of the doctor. They knew, too, that doctors would do everything they could to save them, staying the entire night at their bedside, if required. It is amazing what professional criminals do to their bodies. To prove that he was right, during a fight, an inmate might lift up his shirt, and slice open his stomach with a razor blade or knife. Whoever does this knows that he will be saved when he reaches the hospital. Hospital means paradise where no one works hard other than occasionally carrying water or firewood. And one spends daytime in bed, the greatest break for a Soviet prison camp inmate. In addition there is a great difference in food, sometimes one even receives meat.

Among the criminals some do not have courage to swallow a spoon, tell all about it, and finally lie down on an operating table. They only pretend to be sick. Nobody respects them and they are quickly discovered. If one of these malingerers legitimately fell ill, no one believes them.

Occasionally, madmen among the criminals, the drug addicts, actually gamble with their lives. Since they have no access to drugs, they "borrow" the injection needles from the first-aid station, extract blood from a cat which they inject into themselves. Cat blood does not mix with human blood and the resulting fever gives a pleasant high to the addict. But in conjunction with the inevitable weakening that occurs during the prison stay, even in the strongest bodies, such an experiment can cost a prisoner his life. Still many are willing to try it. Some die, others take their place. They are in a class by themselves. Those who have managed to remain permanently in the hospital regard themselves as the chosen ones.

Normally those working in the hospital have a disease which erupts now and then. There is a twofold reason behind this. First, they do not have to be transported every time they fall ill or get well. Second, the inmates carry out their tasks energetically as long as they are allowed to keep their jobs. In the women's zone several "permanent" hospital workers brought for treatment were allowed to stay until the end of their sentence. However only criminals sentenced under the "normal code" were eligible to work in the hospital. "Especially dangerous prisoners guilty of crimes against the state" and sentenced under the "strict code," were not allowed to work at the hospital, even though this work might be their specialty. For example, a woman doctor could only work as a nurse at the hospital if she was not considered a political prisoner.

Kitchen help, laundry workers, and orderlies were considered "half-well" inmates. On the other hand, women still breastfeeding their babies after giving birth at the hospital, became workhorses, doing all kinds of heavy work, lifting, carrying and digging.

The fire tender's job was not easy. She had to chop the wood for eight stoves, light the stoves, and bring the coal, as well as remove the ashes and carry them out herself. The fire tender while I was there, was a woman in for the tenth time, for theft. About sixty, she had sly, shrewd eyes and vast prison experience. Her bed was in a privileged position, by the window inside the door. It was an unwritten prison law that only thieves sleep at the window. If such a bed ever became free, only a thief would get it.

Despite having lost her left leg, this sixty-year-old woman was a wizard at splitting wood. Her wooden leg was simply a wood block, supporting the stump of the leg at one end and attached to a nailed on rubber boot. She experienced the earth-quake at Ashkhabad, during the quake she fell into a two-year coma. Upon awakening, she no longer had a leg. Her wooden leg thumped loudly upon the floorboards whenever she moved, carrying her heavy load of firewood to the stoves in the doctor's rooms and the inmates' wards. The doctors often praised her industriousness. However, under the prison rules she never received more than ten rubles per month for her hard work. Her bed was in a corner of the ward, where she lived with twenty-nine other sick inmates. She tended the fires on Saturdays and Sundays as on any other day; because days off did not exist. She never complained about needing a rest or lighter work. To the contrary, she appeared pleased with her position. Apparently the concept of freedom did not exist for her nor was she longing for it. She enjoyed teaching her younger colleagues and carried great authority among them. She was more like a mother to the young ones who felt more than respect for her as an older person. The fact that her every word was the law for the younger women gave her an inner pride. She felt as if she had worked her way up through the ranks from private to general. Apparently she belonged to the category of people who, after having spent their entire lives in prison, also expect to die there.

The local tomcat Vasja, "the mailman," gained the love of the entire hospital. Normally he slept in the ward. The inmates loved the tomcat and let him sleep on their pillows. In fact, every one hoped that the tomcat, just in from the yard with muddy paws, would go sleep in her bed. The cat, though no longer young; still carried out his "job" of mail delivery admirably.

The grounds of camp #3 were divided into men's and women's zones, the men's zone much larger than the women's zone. The grounds were divided in direct proportion to the number of forced labor camps in that area, twenty for men and three for women. The hospital zones were separated by a high wooden fence, skirted on each side by a barbed wire fence. Between these fences ran a seven-foot wide, rough-plowed strip. Nobody except the tomcat crossed these barriers since a guard was always on duty in the sentry tower. He prevented anyone from throwing anything across the barbed wire fence. Nobody knew why contact between men and women was so

Tomcat Vasja the "Mailman"

Helene Celmina

closely monitored; it was hard to understand how such contacts could hurt or endanger the state. Before sentencing, strict security made sense, since contacts could influence how an accused person testified at his trial. But in the Mordovian forced labor camps everyone received sentences long ago. If a man called a woman by name, and tossed her a package of cigarettes across the fence, the administration cracked down and made an example of the offenders. The guilty parties were threatened with expulsion from the hospital if they ever repeated their misdeed. Often men called out one of the most common women's names, three women answered, and the guilty one could not be found.

Women who wanted to keep in touch with men did it with the help of the tomcat. He was trained as a kitten to jump across the fence with a note tied to his neck. The tomcat was rewarded with meat from dinner. Working as the hospital's mailman for several years, Vasja knew his job well. In addition, he became adept at distinguishing the free personnel from the prisoners, since the free nurses and doctors chased him out of their beds. Therefore he had become wary of strangers while he loved to sleep in the lap of "his own people."

The great shortage of paper in the Soviet Union was felt within the prison camps where, even a palm-sized piece of old newspaper is of great value, let alone blank paper that can be written upon. Love confessions and promises of eternal faithfulness were written on cigarette pack paper, rolled up and tied around the neck of Vasja the mailman.

Even though the food at the hospital was better than in the camps, one still felt hungry after eating. Potatoes were highly valued and they functioned as a currency to pay for cigarettes, clothing, and even work. Potatoes were carried into the hospital by the breast-feeding mothers who, during the day, loaded potatoes onto railroad cars. The guards at the gate did not confiscate potatoes which were for sale, prices set by mutual agreement. Highest prices were commanded by stockings, cardigans, nail polish, even earrings. I remembered some cheap earrings, a gaudy head scarf, and other trinkets, which I traded for a half a pillowcase of potatoes. The pillowcase was safe during the day since open stealing was not accepted. However, every now and then at night, things disappeared. I checked under the bed whenever I awoke during the night.

The problem was how to boil the potatoes. Once again I received help from the friendly, orderly in for murder. She let me into the nurses' room where nightly I boiled a potato on the electric hot plate. She would not accept a potato as thanks, so I drew her a huge parrot with exotic flowers. My drawings turned out to have value because many women did embroidery in their spare time. Everyone with colored thread asked me to draw something pretty; pictures against payment, naturally. I was offered cigarettes, sugar, and preserved fruit jams. The only problem was getting paper. Some inmates had a good rapport with the doctors or with the free nurses from whom they obtained a few sheets.

One can see the differences between forced labor camps under "strict" and those under "normal" penal codes. In a penal camp under "normal" codes the main problem is not food but finery. For example, dinner in such a camp might be meat broth and mashed potatoes with a sauce. In addition, these inmates received ten rubles a month for shopping. The shops carry cookies, jams, and even shortening. Those with relatives received a five kilogram food parcel once every two months. Whatever else they are legally entitled to, they receive. The law looks after, protects, and preserves them. For all this they are grateful to their Soviet native country, since "where else can man enjoy such freedom?"

As in any hospital, the inmates changed constantly. Most men came to the hospital to rest or to go to the operating room, while the women were seriously ill. A new patient arrived and was taken directly from the gates to the operating room. Our eyes met when she was taken from the operating room to our ward. The left side of her face was bandaged, and when the bandages came off an ugly scar ran from the corner of her left eye to her lower jaw. Whenever she sat in profile so that the scar could not be seen, she had the lovely face of a young girl. But straight on, the scar marred her face so that it was difficult to tell that this was the same girl. My first question to her was, "How old are you?"

"Nineteen."

"Who beautified you like this?"

"I had a girl friend. She became jealous over me talking to someone else and she cut me up."

"What did she cut you with?"

"She sharpened the end of a spoon against the concrete floor. It was as sharp as a knife."

"Wasn't anybody nearby who could have prevented her from doing that?"

"It happened in the living section, everyone was there, but they were scared of her. Luckily my eye and the teeth were untouched. The cheek was cut through completely, reaching the gums."

"Will she be punished for this crime?"

"Not her. What's there to be punished for? I'm alive."

"But she cut you up!"

"I was guilty."

"Why, after all this, do you think that you were guilty?"

"I should have known that while she was friendly with me, I was not allowed to talk with other girls."

"But you're only nineteen! You couldn't have known their rules."

"I couldn't *not* have known them since it's the second time for me."

"How's that? The second time?"

"Well in prison, the second time. And I know everything."

"How old is your girl friend?"

"She's twenty-seven and it's her fourth sentence."

"And what is your face going to look like now? Who's going to marry you?"

"It's going to be good enough for the prison, and no one's going to marry me."

"How much longer do you have to stay inside?"

"Two years and four months."

"How much did you get altogether?"

"Three."

"So you haven't been in very long. How did you find such a wonderful friend in such short time?"

"We got to know each other in the prison cell. I did not want to at first, but she forced me. She showed me the spoon which she used to sharpen every day for at least a half hour."

"But how did you start to talk to someone else?"

"I was taken from the prison and put on the forced labor 'stage.' She was left behind. When she arrived in the camp two months later, she saw that I was eating with somebody else."

"Is that bad, to eat with somebody?"

"Yes. According to our rules, only close friends eat together."

"And you were close friends with the other one?"

"Not yet."

Helene Celmina

"But still you were cut up! And you did not try to defend yourself?"

"It was too late already."

"What was too late?"

"To defend myself."

"Then your girl friend is unpredictable?"

"What's that, unpredictable?"

"Well, it's someone who will do whatever comes to mind, never thinking about the consequences."

"I don't know."

"Tell me frankly, are you angry at your girl friend?"

"No. It was my fault."

"I don't think it was your fault. You never did anything bad."

"I don't know," was the answer. I felt sorry for and angry with this characterless girl. I wanted to tell her that she was stupid. But on the other hand, what had she seen of life and what did she understand?

"Are your parents still living?" I asked.

"My mother is. My father died when my brothers and I were still children."

"How many grades did you finish at school?"

"Nine."

It seemed unbelievable that she could have finished nine grades. I am not sure what the Russian schools teach, but the results are clearly visible. Knowledge is weak, incomplete, and in some cases, totally lacking.

226

CHAPTER 24

BETRAYAL

In the history of the Soviet penal system there has probably never been a camp which did not have its stool pigeons or, as the Russians call them, "stukachi," meaning knockers. These informers usually are people with questionable pasts and moral standings, as well as poor educations. But in camp #17-A the stool pigeon was a young woman recently graduated from an institute of higher learning. She was not Russian with a dark past, but rather a Latvian woman with an enlightened background. At first I was incredulous when several Jehovah's Witnesses told me that my countrywoman Erna passed information to the administration.

There is not a single convict in the Soviet penal camp system whom the administration has not tried to recruit as an informer. This does not happen during the first days, but after about a year of captivity when the relationships with other prisoners have developed and certain things have been learned. Then the proposal comes quite unexpectedly.

Camp #17-A was visited weekly by a Cheka representative named Yershov. A black-haired Russian of medium build, about forty, Yershov carried himself with self assurance. As he walked through the gate toward his office, he seemed unaware of people, however, he saw everyone. Everyone realized Yershov was dangerous and remained on their guard when talking to him. As he spoke, his face became distorted by a false grin which continued throughout the conversation.

One Friday he ordered a whole list of women to his office. There were about twelve of us, mostly Jehovah's Witnesses, waiting in a long line in the corridor. My turn came. I knocked and walked in. Yershov sat behind a desk and, assuming his best false smile and addressed me by my first name. This is not the normal style of address in a Soviet prison. The informality immediately put me on guard, but I tried to appear witless and asked: "How do you know my first name?"

"You should realize that it is my duty to know all about you, and to take care of you."

"That is odd," I said, "What do you want from me?"

"I don't want anything, but I would like to help you."

"To help me personally, or all of us here at the camp?"

"This time I am talking about you personally. I would like to relieve your present situation."

"How?"

"I would like you to understand me correctly. A lot depends on me; I can allow you to receive food parcels from your relatives, and for two rubles a month you will be able to buy something at the store."

"Thank you for your kindness, but I don't have the money for the store, and for a ruble a month I won't be able to buy anything anyway. What do you want in return?"

"Oh, you are cunning," he pretended to be laughing at a joke.

"Well, we are living in times when nobody does anything for nothing."

Yershov made a somber face and continued. "You understand everything, but you don't realize that this can have an adverse effect on you and your future."

"What has this got to do with my future. I am serving a sentence completely without reason, and when it is finished, then goodbye to you and to everybody else."

"But what about my reference?"

"What sort of reference do I need from you? I spit on that kind of reference."

"But do you understand correctly what I have asked of you?"

"That I should bring you information about the other prisoners."

"That's not quite so, you have misunderstood me. I would like you to speak with the Jehovah's Witnesses and find the main leaders."

"As a service for you?"

"You see only evil in our work, but you don't understand that we work to keep people out of prisons."

"I laugh at your noble words. Why do you need the main leaders?"

"That's because, well, you know yourself that most of them are uneducated and stupid, and they would have been sent home long ago if they had been willing to regret their breaches of the law. But their main leaders don't permit it, and that's why they sit in camp. If you would find their leaders, think of the benefits for the others and yourself. First, many of them would be released before their time, and second, you could receive food from home. And, maybe you will be released sooner also!"

With his last words, the Chekist assumed his glued-on smile. I understood his strategy. The older leaders would be taken to Vladimir Prison, and the other Jehovah's Witnesses would be worked over one by one to force them to renounce their faith.

I announced loudly and with irony, "If you have decided to trust this important mission to me, you have made a mistake. I

Helene Celmina

am not the right one for such assignments which amount to betrayal."

"But maybe you will change your mind?"

"No."

"You may go." Nothing remained of his grin and his words fell like the blows of an ax. When I was at the door, he reminded me to call in the next woman.

The next in line was one of the leaders of the Jehovah's Witnesses. I embraced her in the hallway and whispered "Brace yourself!" in her ear. She was kept in the office for at least two hours.

On following Fridays I began to observe who was called to Yershov's office. Most often it was Erna. I noticed that Erna acquired lipstick which she wore when she went to the office. Presumably, from Erna's painted lips flowed the names of women about whom there was something to report. Anyone else in her place I would have pitied, since her work was not pleasant, but it did not enter my mind to pity Erna after watching how proudly she opened the outer door of the administration building. She galled me immensely and my anger grew, but without concrete facts, I could say nothing.

Still, I asked, and once said to her quite innocently, "I have noticed that you walk over to Yershov's office frequently. What does he want with you?"

"Nothing in particular. He says I should help the boys."

"What boys?"

"The ones I was tried with."

"Have you gone out of your mind? Or maybe he has. How could you help them now? They have been convicted, and received long sentences."

"Don't say that! I can do it."

"Wait a minute. There is something I don't understand. It's turning out that Yershov is some kind of benefactor rather than a Cheka agent?"

"That's how it is turning out."

"Then maybe you can tell me in more detail how you can help them. Maybe we should sit down." We walked to the nearest bench and Erna started her story.

"Yershov told me about every one of our boys, how hard they have to work and so on. He said that some of them could go home right away if they would write a letter of regret which could be published in the newspaper. After a short time, the sentence would be lifted."

"Let him talk to them himself. Why does he get you involved in their affairs?"

"It concerns Uldis. He knows I like Uldis."

"How can he know that?"

"When they were all discussed, one after the other, he mentioned Uldis also."

"And you, of course, blurted out that you like him."

"And what's bad about that? Yes, I did blurt that out. Now I will be able to help Uldis."

"That's interesting! How?"

"You see, it was only to my advantage that I told about Uldis. Now I have permission to write to him at the men's camp."

"Oho!" I was surprised.

"And Yershov gave me Uldis' brother's name and address in Riga. His brother is still young and goes to secondary school."

"What do you need his address for?"

"Why not, I have to persuade Uldis' brother to ask Uldis to stop resisting stubbornly and to regret everything. I already sent the text of the letter which his brother has to send to Uldis."

"And Yershov dictated this text to you?"

"I wrote the text, only the idea came from him."

Uldis is an adult and knows how to behave. Maybe he won't like this. If he is, as you say, resisting stubbornly, then he must know what he is doing."

"You don't understand anything," Erna said angrily.

"Maybe." Seeing that this subject was closed, I walked away.

Occasionally my suspicions concerning Erna's visits recurred, but one day I learned the facts. Another Latvian woman received a visit from her daughter. This woman had arrived in camp #17-A about six months earlier on a two years sentence because an acquaintance, a Latvian poet gave her his handwritten book of patriotic poems to read. The woman's apartment was searched, the poems were found, and they were both convicted: The poet for writing, and the woman for reading. She was accused of anti-Soviet agitation. She received two years in a strict regime labor camp, while the author received seven years, also in strict regime labor. Because there are no strict regime labor camps in Latvia, she made the long trip to Mordovia. Her name was Rute. Although, compared to the other women, Rute was in the camp only a short time, her joy at her daughter's visit was immense. When she first heard about it, she flushed with excitement and said, "Where did the child get the money for such a long trip?"

Railroad travel in the Soviet Union is cheap compared to that in other countries. Rute told me earlier that she did not suffer as much from the incarceration as from the thought that her teenage daughters were left without any means of support. Nothing at home could be sold, and the girls were still going to school and were too young to work. Rute had a hard life because her husband died young, leaving her with three children. She worked as a bookkeeper earning eighty rubles a month, and she managed to support her family with her small vegetable garden plot near Riga. The children carried water in buckets from a ditch. Then her son, the eldest, married, and Rute was left with the two girls until her arrest. It was the older daughter, already in her last year in high school, who suddenly arrived. Although Rute worried about the shortage of money at home, the joy of seeing her daughter overshadowed her concern. Rute was led out of the penal zone to the small visitor's cottage to meet her daughter.

Toward the evening of the next day, Ona, who worked in the ambulance, called me aside and said anxiously, "Rute is in a bad way. I gave her an injection, my last two ampules. If she needs more during the night I will have nothing to give her."

"Did she get bad news from home?"

"No, not that. It is much worse."

"What could be worse?"

"Betrayal."

"Betrayal?" I repeated, confused.

"Yes, treachery. Erna has betrayed her."

"In what way, and for what?"

Helene Celmina

"Well listen. Rute received a ten ruble note from her daughter. She did not want to take it, because of the poverty in which her girls live. But the daughter insisted that she receives help from the brother. Rute hid the money which was not found during the search upon leaving the visitor's cottage. After walking through the gate into the penal zone, Rute met Erna and joyfully told her everything. Erna apparently rushed to the guard shack, because two guards came and rifled through Rute's bed until they found the money hidden in a pillowcase. The other beds were not touched. Rute collapsed next to her bed. Valya ran to me and told me what had happened, and we ran to the barracks and carried Rute to the infirmary."

I felt a lump in my throat. I expected anything from Erna but that. The women had warned me long ago. "I will drag this snake into the daylight," I muttered indignantly.

"Just don't do anything rash. Don't do anything that will get you more years because of that slut."

"No, no, don't worry about me. I am going to drag her into the light with everybody watching. Is she so stupid to think that nobody will find out? How is she going to face Rute?"

"You know, I don't understand it either, and have never been able to."

Later, when I saw Erna pumping water, I walked up and asked directly "Can you tell me why you are betraying other prisoners?"

"She did not lose composure, did not even blink. She straightened up like a cobra before attacking its victim and chopped her words, "It is the duty of every conscientious Soviet citizen."

These words numbed my mind and I could only ask, "But how then did you, the conscientious one, happen to get in here?"

Erna said only, "I got here and that's all."

I walked to the barracks, determined to warn everyone about Erna, the sooner, the better.

My section of the barracks was active because the second shift was preparing to leave for work. The clothing factory worked two shifts, the day shift from morning until five, and the evening shift until one in the morning. Some of the women stepped outside. One was darning her completely worn out dress, another one was writing a letter to her relatives. Some close enough to the light were reading. It was quiet in the barracks. Erna reclined on her cot and paged through a magazine. I felt the moment had arrived.

I pulled myself together and went to the long table in the middle of the section. Pressing my palms against the table edge for support, I said, "Women, listen! There is a dangerous traitor among us; she will spare nobody. If any of you have secrets, keep them hidden so she won't be able to betray you."

The eyes of the women riveted upon me. Some were not surprised since they knew it already, but those who heard it for the first time were greatly taken aback. "Who is she?," exploded from all sides.

After a short dramatic pause, I pointed at Erna, and said, "There she is. My countrywoman Erna." I drank a glass of water because my hands trembled.

The quiet of the section was replaced by loud conversation as nearly every woman spoke to her nearest roommate or sister-in-faith. Not the least concerned, Erna continued to look through her magazine as if she did not care what people were saying. That's how confident she was. My words were like water rolling off a duck's back. This event was discussed in the camp for several days. There had been many previous cases of suspicion, but never had they been discussed as openly as I dared to. I received many words of thanks, and several women embraced and kissed me.

I never spoke to Erna again. Through others she tried to renew normal relations with me, but I refused.

Fortunately, Rute recovered without any serious consequences. She did not know who had betrayed her in Riga when her house was searched for the poetry book. She did however, know who betrayed her in captivity about the hidden ten rubles. In less than a year, Rute's term was up and she was released. None of us learned if she told her children about the betrayal in the camp. Perhaps not because she was an exceptionally sensitive person who wanted to shield her children.

After Rute left, everything remained as before in the camp. On Fridays, Yershov arrived. Erna visited him and continued to do her duty as a conscientious Soviet citizen, not regarding it as treachery. Finally, Erna stopped sleeping in her bunk during the nights when Vanya was on guard duty. According to regulations, no one was allowed to leave the barracks during the night. Erna must have been convinced that none of the women would turn her in. She was right. No one did.

CHAPTER 25

EPILOGUE

It was a warm, sunny day in Moscow on June 10, 1966. In Alexander Park, near the walls of the Kremlin, flowers bloomed. People walked on the footpaths, others sat on the park benches. I also sat on one of the benches, enjoying the flowers and the sunny day. It seemed that nothing had changed, everything was as it was four years ago, except the women's dresses were shorter.

Five or six men in military uniforms walked towards me. Suddenly, I felt a shortness of breath and my heart pounded like a sledgehammer. The pulse in my temples banged, and my hands trembled. Only after the military men passed me and disappeared behind the green shrubbery at the end of the path, did my heart gradually return to normal. The same fear and anxiety gripped me a short while later when I saw two policemen, walking on a distant footpath. Like the military men, they never even looked in my direction. I told myself that I had no cause for fear. I had received a release and a picture showing that I served my sentence.

My first day in freedom was a strange, unusual sensation. On the train it was still hard to grasp, but getting off, the surroundings overwhelmed me, and I wasn't sure which way to turn. Since no loving soul waited in Riga, I decided to spend a few days with acquaintances in Moscow. Because my feet were not used to walking on asphalt, now and then I sat down to rest. Although I sat by the Kremlin wall, my thoughts lingered with those who were left behind in camp #17-A. Those women belonged to various nationalities and their appearances were as diverse as their life stories, but one classification united them: Prisoner. Only the lengths of their terms of imprisonment differed.

How many did not belong there at all? Did anyone besides their friends and relatives know anything about them? It occurred to me that people should know about them. I decided to tell everyone, wherever I went, about the unfortunate women prisoners, what they had done, and how they had been convicted. I wanted to write all of it down so that over the years I would not forget. At the thought of writing, I feared I was about to commit a serious crime against the state. For describing the life stories of these unfortunate women, I would be subject, according to Section II, paragraph sixty-five of the Criminal code of Soviet Latvia, to ten years of incarceration. How I wanted to write! My anxiety grew. This must be the same anxiety felt by professional criminals preparing to commit a new crime. I decided that the planning of my new crime must be postponed for a while. In the distance I noticed more military personnel and became scared again, as if I had already committed the new crime.

Months passed, and every time I thought again about writing, my anxiety returned. The fear which gripped me upon seeing military people or policemen tortured me for several years. As my fear ebbed, I began my story with "Clara." Later I added other notes. In June of 1977, when my apartment was again searched and the assistant prosecutor of the city of Riga minutely examined every sliver of paper, all the notes were discovered. I was asked afterwards, both by the prosecutor and by the Cheka where the other chapters were, since the story about Clara was designated "Chapter Eight." No one believed me when I said that there were none. I abandoned my writing indefinitely because of the Cheka's great interest in my apartment. After having gained my freedom in the West, I immediately sat down to write my book. May those unfortunate women about whom I have forgotten to write, forgive me.

Helene Celmina

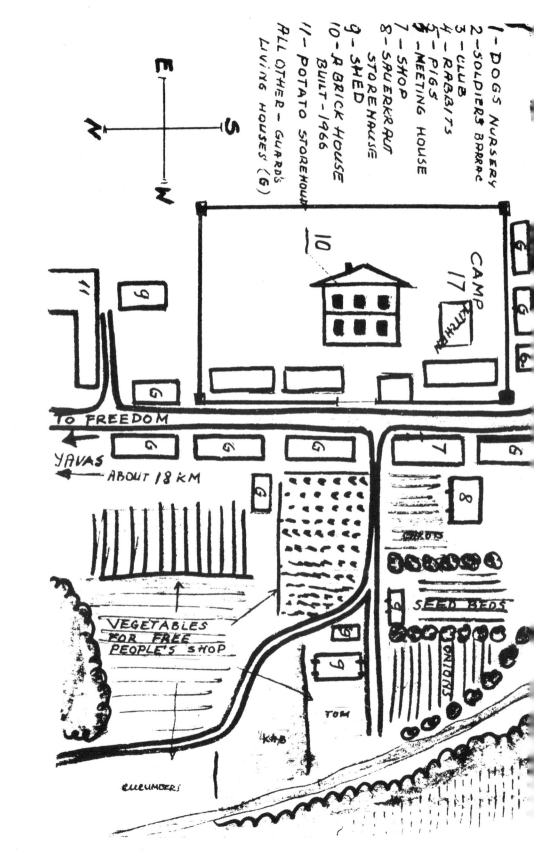

1 — DOGS NURSERY
2 — SOLDIERS BARRAC
3 — CLUB
4 — RABBITS
5 — PIGS
6 — MEETING HOUSE
7 — SHOP
8 — SAUERKRAUT STOREHOUSE
9 — SHED
10 — A BRICK HOUSE BUILT 1966
11 — POTATO STOREHOUSE
ALL OTHER — GUARDS LIVING HOUSES (G)

N
E
S
W

CAMP 17

10

G

G

G

G

TO FREEDOM

YAVAS
ABOUT 18 KM

G   G   G

G

7

6

8

CARROTS

SEED BEDS

9   9

ONIONS

VEGETABLES
FOR FREE
PEOPLE'S SHOP

TOM

KAB

CUCUMBERS